px.

10

Poems Without Names

Poems Without Names

RAYMOND OLIVER

The English Lyric,
1200–1500

UNIVERSITY OF CALIFORNIA PRESS

Berkeley, Los Angeles, London 1970

University of California Press
Berkeley and Los Angeles, California

University of California Press, Ltd.
London, England

Copyright © 1970 by
The Regents of the University of California

Standard Book Number: 520–01403–0
Library of Congress Catalog Card Number: 77–82617
Design by Dave Comstock
Printed in the United States of America

To
Mary Anne,
"An hendy hap"

Contents

Preface

his book is an anthology as well as a study of short poems in Middle English. I have interlarded my prose with eighty-six medieval lyrics quoted in full, mainly to illustrate arguments but also to render these little-known poems more accessible (see the Index of First Lines, which also gives references to the original manuscript and standard edition of each poem). In choosing these poems from among the twelve or thirteen hundred that I examined, I have tried to present the Middle English tradition in the best possible light. I do not pretend that the poems I have chosen are all masterpieces; but I do think that each of them has some particular distinction, and I have always picked the best one I could find to support my argument.

Among the many debts I have incurred in writing this book, I would like to acknowledge a few by name. Professors Yvor Winters and Wesley Trimpi taught me, in person, most of what I know about the reading and writing of poetry; without them, I would not have had the equipment to deal with individual poems. Professor R. W. Ackerman, who directed the book when it was a dissertation, supported me with encouragement and tolerance, gave me a great deal of help with historical background, language, and bibliography, and started the whole enterprise by introducing me, very genially, to medieval English studies. Professor V. A. Kolve, besides carefully reading the manuscript in dissertation form, has provided me, in his writing and his Stanford seminar on medieval drama, with a model of historical and literary scholarship. Professors Josephine Miles, J. V. Cunningham, and Fred C. Robinson have all commented with great intelligence and generosity on this manuscript in various stages of its writing; I have made nearly all the changes and additions they suggested. To Mr. Gene Tanke, of the U. C. Press, I owe such debts as one owes to a skillful and sympathetic midwife; without his help, the baby might have been still-born. And to my wife, Mary Anne Oliver, who has spent countless hours typing the manuscript and very subtly criticizing it from a dozen points of view, I owe a very great debt.

I would like to thank the trustees of the Leverhulme Foundation for their financial support during the first year of my research on the medieval lyric.

I would also like to give thanks to the following publishers for permission to quote from these copyrighted books: Bantam Books, Inc., *The Complete Works of François Villon*; the Clarendon Press, Oxford, *English Lyrics of the 13th Century, Religious Lyrics of the 14th Century, Religious Lyrics of the 15th Century, Secular Lyrics of the 14th and 15th Centuries, The Early English Carols*, and *The Oxford Nursery Rhyme Book*; the Columbia University Press, *The Exeter Book, The Anglo-Saxon Minor Poems*, and *Historical Poems of the XIVth and XVth Centuries*; Walter De Gruyter and Co., *Die Gedichte Walthers von der Vogelweide*; Harcourt, Brace, and World, Inc., *Ceremony and Other Poems* (copyright 1948 by Richard Wilbur, first published in *The New Yorker*); Liveright Publishing Corp., *Complete Poems and Selected Letters of Hart Crane*; New Directions Publishing Corp., *Personae* (copyright 1927 by Ezra Pound); Oxford University Press, *Poems and Prose of Gerard Manley Hopkins*; Penguin Books, Ltd., *The Penguin Book of Latin Verse*; Random House, Inc., and Alfred A. Knopf, Inc., *Poems and Essays* by John Crowe Ransom, and *The Collected Poems of Wallace Stevens*; Routledge and Kegan Paul, Ltd., and Harvard University Press, *The Collected Poems of Sir Thomas Wyatt*, and *The Poems of Sir Walter Raleigh*; *The Southern Review*, "The Progress of the Feast" by Raymond Oliver; the Swallow Press, Inc., *The Exclusions of a Rhyme* by J. V. Cunningham, and *Collected Poems* by Yvor Winters; the University of Washington Press, *Cambridge Middle English Lyrics*; the World Publishing Co., *New Poets of England and America*; and the Yale University Press, *Minor Poems* by Alexander Pope.

A Note on Middle English

ince this book is for general readers of poetry as well as students of medieval literature, some brief comments on the language of the texts should be helpful. I have not changed that language, as it appears in the standard editions, except to replace the misleading runic symbol Þ ("wynn") with its modern equivalent, *w*.

The following are variant forms or spellings of common words:

1. Initial *h* may be dropped or added: *is* = "his;" *hut* = *ut* = "out."
2. The first person pronoun "I" may also appear as *ic, ich* or one of their variants (*yc, ik*, etc.).
3. The conjunction "if" also occurs as *yf, yif, ʒif, gif.*
4. Common contractions with the negative particle *ne* are *nis* (*ne is* = "is not") and *not* (*ne wot* = "don't know," first and third person singular).
5. The auxiliary "shall" also occurs as *scal, sal*, and *ssal.*

Some of these variations, and some of the variations in grammar and spelling discussed below, indicate differences in dialect. For the purpose of studying the lyrics, the two main dialect areas are Northern (including the North East Midlands and England north of the Humber) and Southern (including the West and South East Midlands, Kent, and the southeastern portion of England). Among the important dialect features of these two broad areas, again with reference to the lyrics only, are the following: the auxiliary "shall" is *sal* in the North, *shall* in the South; the ending of the present indicative, third person singular, is -*es* in the North (*falles*) and -eth in the South (*falleþ*); and the personal pronoun in the third person plural is *them* in the North, *hem* in the South.

A number of grammatical features that distinguish Middle from Modern English are especially prominent in the lyrics:

1. infinitives in -e/-en (*synge, stonden*)
2. past participles with a y-/i- prefix (*i-blessyd*)
3. present indicative, third person singular in -*eth* (*beginneþ*)
4. "to have" in the present indicative, third person plural may be *han*

5. the feminine personal pronoun may be either *she* (a Northern form) or *he/hi*, or a variant

6. the personal pronoun and adjective, third person plural, may be either *they/them/their* or *hi/hem/hire* or a variant.

Although Middle English poets used several letters no longer in our alphabet, their spelling confuses us mainly because it is inconsistent. The unfamiliar letters are þ, called "thorn," used interchangeably with ð, called "eth"; and ȝ, called "yogh." Both occur most frequently in the earlier texts. The þ/ð (þ is more common than ð) represents the modern *th* sound, voiced or unvoiced, as in *þonc* ("thought") and *þanne* ("then"). The ȝ represents several sounds, depending largely on its position: initially, it is like the modern *y*, as in *ȝonge* ("young"); medially or finally, it was pronounced like the German *ch* in either *ich* or *ach*, depending on its phonetic environment (*myȝt* is like German *ich*, *cauȝte* is like *ach*); in final position, and sometimes medially, it could also be pronounced like the modern *z* or *s* (*turneȝ*, "turns"). The sounds represented by medial ȝ were also spelled with *h*: *þoht* ("thought"), *fiht* ("fight").

The following is a list of common variants in spelling:

1. s/z: *zuo* = "so"
2. sh/ch, sh/x: *che* = "she"; *xuld* = "should"
3. t/th: *wit* = "with"
4. v/f, v/w, v/u, f/u: *hafe* = "have"; *himselwen* = "himselven"; *luue* = "love"; *euery* = "every"; *uram* = "from"
5. w/wh/qu/qw: *quat* = "what"; *qwa* = "who"
6. i as j: *ioye* = "joy"; *ihesu* = "Jesus"
7. i/y/u/e: *synne* = "sin;" *sunne* = "sin"; *senful* = "sinful"
8. ou/ow: *ȝowre* = "your"
9. u/o: *sonne* = "sun"

In general, it is well to remember that pronouncing Middle English aloud (correctly) will aid comprehension. Correct pronunciation may be encouraged, in turn, by remembering that Middle English vowels had not yet been diphthongized, and therefore sounded much like the vowels of modern Spanish or Italian. And until the fifteenth century, most of the letters were pronounced, including final *e*. The best procedure is probably to learn Chaucer's pronunciation—see, for example, Helge Kökeritz's *Guide to Chaucer's Pronunciation*—and then apply it to the Middle English lyric.

In glossing the medieval poems, I have usually not repeated matters explained in this Note. I have also assumed a general acquaintance with Middle English, such as may be acquired by reading most of Chaucer. Thus I have not tried to explain all of the countless differences between medieval and modern English (for instance, ME *meat* does not mean "meat"), but have glossed only the more difficult words and phrases.

Abbreviations

13th:	*English Lyrics of the Thirteenth Century*, ed. Carleton Brown (Oxford, 1932)
14th:	*Religious Lyrics of the XIVth Century*, ed. Carleton Brown, 2nd ed. rev. G. V. Smithers (Oxford, 1924), corrected reprint 1957.
15th:	*Religious Lyrics of the XVth Century*, ed. Carleton Brown (Oxford, 1939).
14/15th:	*Secular Lyrics of the XIVth and XVth Centuries*, ed. Rossell Hope Robbins, 2d ed. (Oxford, 1955).
B.M.:	British Museum, London.
C:	*The Early English Carols*, ed. Richard Leighton Greene (Oxford, 1935).
Cam.:	*Cambridge Middle English Lyrics*, ed. Henry A. Person (Seattle, 1962).
Camb.:	Cambridge.
F:	"The Findern Anthology," ed. Rossell Hope Robbins, *PMLA* 49 (June 1954): 610–642.
HP:	*Historical Poems of the XIVth and XV Centuries*, ed. Rossell Hope Robbins (New York, 1959).
LL:	R. M. Wilson, *The Lost Literature of Medieval England* (London, 1952): 187.
MS(S):	Manuscript(s).
OEM:	*An Old English Miscellany*, ed. Richard Morris, EETS, No. 49 (London, 1872): 100.
Pr:	"Popular Prayers in Middle English Verse," ed. Rossell Hope Robbins, *MP* 36(May 1939): 337–350.
Wall Verses:	"Wall Verses at Launceston Priory," ed. Rossell Hope Robbins, *Archiv für das Studium der Neueren Sprachen und Literaturen* 200(1963): 338–343.

Poems Without Names

1. Theory and Method

The whole corpus of Middle English lyrics, written between about 1200 and 1500, has a high degree of stylistic coherence; and this coherence derives from the anonymous, practical, and public nature of the poems.[1] I believe, in fact, that these poems, written over a period of three hundred years by a very large number of people,* have as much formal unity as the complete works of certain modern poets, such as Yeats, who change their style in the course of a long career, and more unity than the work of a few extremely versatile and long-lived poets, such as Goethe. To illustrate:

A. Of euerykune° tre—   *every kind of*
    of euerykune tre—
  þe haweþorn blowet° suotes°   *blossoms; sweetest*
4   of euerykune tre.

  My lemmon° sse ssal boe—°   *beloved; be*
    my lemmon sse ssal boe—
  þe fairest of erþkinne,°   *"earth-kind"*
8   my lemmon sse ssal boe.

B. Naueþ my saule bute fur and ys.   *My soul has nothing but fire and ice*
    and þe lichome° eorþe and treo.°   *body; wood*
  [B]idde we alle þen heye kyng.   *Let us all pray the high king*
4   þat welde schal þe laste dom.   *that shall wield the Last Judgment*
  þat he vs lete° þat ilke° þing.°   *spare; same; (doom)*
    þat we mowen his wille don.   *that we may do his will*
  He vs skere of þe tyþing.   *May he excuse us from the tithing*
8   þat sunfule schulle an-vnderfon.   *that sinners should receive*
  Hwenne deþ heom lat to þe Murehþe[1]
    þat neuer ne byþ undon.

                Amen.

---

* Since the general forms or structures of these poems do not essentially change in the course of three hundred years, my study will not be concerned with chronology and development.

[1] *When death leads them to the Mirth*

The first is a simple love song from the fourteenth century.* Since the poet's "lemmon" could be anyone's, anyone could use this song to celebrate his sweetheart and gain her favor; no detail is particularized, and there is no private psychological content. The second is a thirteenth-century mortality poem, in which "my" and "we" both refer to Everyman, and which was written to bring about Everyman's repentance. Both poems, opposite in mood, are equally general, anonymous, and useful; and they show an appropriate unity of style, in the coincidence of syntax and metrical line, in the use of simple balanced contrasts (hawthorn—sweetheart, body—soul, fire and ice—earth and wood), in their sparsely modified nouns and verbs, and in other traits of style suitable for oral delivery.

This unity is deep and distinct, but also various; it embraces a good many different kinds of poem. To establish a broad basis for generalizations, I have therefore isolated ten major categories and drawn a number of examples from each of them: drinking and feast songs, popular love poems, satires, practical and occasional verse, courtly love poems, Marian poems, Christmas carols and songs,† Passiontide and Easter poems, moral and didactic verse (mostly in the *contemptus mundi* tradition), and a loose assortment of devotional and theological poems.

My method is to find and analyze general forms or principles of order shared by poems in most or all of the ten categories; and my purpose in doing this is to define the tradition of the anonymous short poem in Middle English. Insofar as a tradition in this sense is marked by stylistic and structural devices occurring together, in poem after poem, over a period of time, the twelve or thirteen hundred anonymous lyrics I have surveyed make up a single tradition. By "stylistic and structural devices" I mean all elements that modify the total effect of the lyric, from local, linguistic devices such as alliteration, to large, structural principles such as a narrative plot. These principles of order (conventions, general forms) thus permeate the entire body of a poem,

---

* Poems mentioned or discussed in the text are cited according to the numbers they have in their standard editions; for example, "13th: 6" refers to the sixth poem in *English Lyrics of the Thirteenth Century*, ed. Carleton Brown. For the complete list of abbreviations and editions, see p. xv.

† I have concentrated on Christmas carols because they seem to represent the whole genre adequately, at least as far as structure is concerned.

affecting words, phrases, sentences, stanzas, and the poem as a whole; they do not include phonemes, morphemes, variant inflectional forms and spellings, and other such units which may concern the linguist but do not function stylistically.

My task, then, is, in the words of J. V. Cunningham, "to describe the rules of the game." Cunningham, whose essays have provided the essential method of my study, has himself concisely described this kind of literary analysis:

> The rules of poetry, or rather the rules of the various traditions of poetry, are of the same order [as the rules governing syllogisms and chess], but even more complex. Nevertheless, they are describable, and to describe the rules of the game is to define a tradition. A tradition is all the ways a particular poem could have been written; it is the potentiality of realized structures, as the rules of chess contain all the games that may be played. . . . Hence, the notions which constitute a tradition are not ideas merely, but principles of order. They are schemes which direct the production of works. For a principle of order is that which directs and determines the selection of the materials that enter into a work, and their succession and importance. Such principles may relate to language as such. Meter and rhyme are of this sort, and so is what we ordinarily call language. A poem in Latin is not a poem in English. But even within a given language there are many sublanguages, and there have been in all periods of the history of poetry special selections of language appropriated to poems, or to certain kinds of poems, or to certain groups of poets.[2]

Thus, from another point of view, my task is to write the grammar of a poetic sublanguage—a historical grammar, since I am concerned with what the poems mean in their own terms. The general principles of order which the poems share, and which consequently define their tradition, may be roughly divided into two classes: those that affect the meaning of words, phrases, and whole poems (diction, imagery, metaphor and other figures, tone), and those that bind these parts together (figures of sound, meter and rhythm, overall structures). The first of these groups corresponds loosely to semantics, the second to syntax.

But I do not propose a purely formal and descriptive study, on the model of a traditional Germanic grammar. As I have said, I am concerned with the *intentions* of the medieval poems. It has been argued lately that "historical reconstruction" is difficult and (there-

5

fore?) perhaps undesirable.[3] Of course a critic may devise private interpretations, more or less artfully, with slight concern for the original
meaning of the text; but I would like to avoid this. My ideal is the old
and now unfashionable ideal of historical philology, which J. V. Cunningham, once again, has succinctly restated: "A work of art is the
embodiment of an intention. To realize an intention in language is the
function of the writer. To realize from language the intention of the
author is the function of the reader or the critic, and his method is
historical or philological interpretation."[4]

To this I would add that in medieval literature, at least, we have
nothing but the embodiment of the intention; there is no temptation to
discuss the text apropos of the private experience and mental work-
ings of its author, a dubious enterprise even where modern poetry is
concerned. Also, "intention" is in many cases a less appropriate word
than "purpose" or "function." In my usage, and in common usage as
well, these three words may be located on a scale of ascending deliberateness or self-consciousness, with intention at the top and function at
the bottom, although intention and purpose tend to be interchangeable
in certain contexts. But purpose is in general more broad and less
calculated than intention.[5] I shall use "function" to indicate relevance
to a larger purpose or intention; a word, for instance, may function in
a verse, a verse in a poem, and a poem in a formal celebration with
music, dancing, and the like.

In all my attempts to define what a poem was meant to do or say,
I am interested in what Isabel Hungerland calls the "life function" of
the poem, as distinct from its "linguistic function": "[the latter] concerns what we want to do with language—make statements, appraise,
command, question; [the former] concerns what we want to do by
means of the language function exhibited."[6] To ascertain the life function of language spoken to us in conversation, we take into account the
speaker's tone of voice, gestures, facial expressions, the situation in
which he is speaking, and our personal knowledge of him. Thus we
gauge his meaning on the basis of probability, with the attendant risk
of misunderstanding, unless his words are quite explicit and rather simple. But to grasp the life function of a poem, we have only the bare text
and a body of more or less relevant contemporary evidence, in the form
of other documents, pictures, historical facts, and so forth. Our reading
of the text, like the result of a legal process, is, then, only probable and

circumstantial; and we admit none but medieval evidence to the extent that we are interested in the poem's meaning rather than our own.* I realize that Marxist and Freudian readings of past literature may be illuminating or diverting, but they do not illuminate the medieval past *in its own terms*, even if we believe that the Spirit of these men is present in all times and places. Fortunately, we have no need of such special help in order to interpret the Middle English lyrics, because most of their original meaning is, as a matter of fact, quite explicit and rather simple.

In discussing the intentions and original meanings of lyric poems, I have used a hidden assumption: that poems and persons are comparable. I think this assumption is reasonable, on the grounds that poems, like persons, can speak to us and therefore express intentions, which presumably coincide with the authors' intentions, though not necessarily. The crux of historical interpretation is the act of comprehending otherness in a poem, and this is very much like comprehending another person. Both acts are mysterious, and both are of the greatest importance:

> the principle apparently holds that, in a valid but not exclusive sense, each work of art is not only an object but a kind of surrogate for a person. Anything that bids for attention in an act of contemplation is a surrogate for a person. In proportion as the work of art is capable of being taken in full seriousness, it moves further and further along an asymptote to the curve of personality.[7]

My method is comparative as well as historical: I find it helpful, in illuminating a few specific points, to contrast medieval poetry with some modern English poems written between about 1865 and 1965; and I shall conclude by relating the Middle English lyric to several other poetic traditions. Anything, from God to poetry, will be understood better if we understand what it is not.

Intention is of crucial importance because it is the raison d'être

* Of course our own minds must contribute to the process of reading a poem; but our specifically modern contribution to the total meaning should be schematic or formal, not thematic. That is, we may bring to the text a modern technical apparatus for analyzing its parts—the diction, the arrangement of words, the overall structure, and so on—but we should not insert modern themes and intentions into the text (Oedipus complex, exploitation of the working class) at the risk of perverting what the poems are meant to say. Whatever formal structures we may find in a poem are implicit, whereas Freudian and other twentieth-century meanings are superimposed.

of the poem, and it determines the poem's shape. I realize that form, conversely, is a way of discovering meanings, thus intentions; but intention remains the Aristotelean first cause of the poem, and its soul, its principle of life. The three main intentions of the Middle English lyric are to celebrate, to persuade, and to define. But these differences of intention do not alter the basic oneness of the medieval lyric, because their unity is, first of all, formal. The poems share certain kinds of diction, metaphor, overall structure, and other general forms that cut across differences among the three intentions, just as, in speaking German, one uses the same kinds of grammar, syntax, and pronunciation to say entirely different things. The differences among celebrating, persuading, and defining are semantic rather than formal.

The principal reason why these three intentions do not disturb the oneness of the tradition is that they do not "say entirely different things." All three of them, as they occur in Middle English poems, are essentially public, practical, and anonymous; and these are their most distinctive qualities. The poems are meant to affect the lives of large classes of people, not to express the delights and agonies of unique, post-Romantic souls. But this is common knowledge. Albert C. Baugh, in his history of Middle English literature, has defined certain general traits of Middle English literature which are at the same time "characteristic of all medieval literature." First, it is impersonal: medieval poets—often friars or other clerics—were anonymous;[8] "the reproduction of books by hand tended to give [the books] in time a communal character" (scribes altered the manuscripts); and the Middle Ages did not value originality. Second, the presence of women in the audience goes far towards explaining the courtly or semi-courtly tone of many poems. In the third place, "one is constantly aware in medieval literature of the all-important place of the Church in medieval life"; fourth, "even where religion is not directly concerned, a moral purpose is frequently discernible in literature, openly avowed or tacitly implied as the justification for its existence"; finally, and especially important for the style of the short poem, "much of literature until near the end of the Middle Ages was meant to be listened to rather than read," which meant that verse, because it is easy to remember, was very widely used.[9] All of these ingredients, in different proportions, have combined to give the Middle English poems their plain, homebrewed flavor. It is my purpose in studying them to define this

8

flavor and thus lend precision to the commonplaces I have quoted from Baugh.

Closely involved with the oral, public nature of the lyrics is their rhetorical or, in a broad sense, grammatical basis. Rhetorical figures occur in these poems, as they occur in any literature;[10] but we need not assume that the poets learned them from the rhetoric manuals of Geoffroi de Vinsauf, Matthieu de Vendôme, John of Garland, or some other *Ars versificatoria* of the twelfth or thirteenth century. Recent studies by James J. Murphy show that formal rhetoric was apparently not studied earlier than 1431 in English universities, and not earlier than the fifteenth century in the lower schools.[11] But the nameless poets, whoever they were, must have received some kind of literary education, though very few would have gone to a university, since practically no one did in those days. There is no doubt that most of the poets attended a cathedral school, monastic school, or some kind of urban public school, except for those few that studied with individual masters.[12] Instruction from any of these sources would have relied on standard works of grammar like the *Ars maior* and *Ars minor* of Donatus, the *Graecismus* of Evrard de Béthune, or the *De grammatica* of Priscian. All of these books, as well as the rhetoric manuals, deal with the same tropes and figures and other devices that we find in the anonymous lyrics:[13] metaphor (*translatio*), allegory (*permutatio*), the proverb (*sententia*), the illustrative story (*exemplum*), antithesis (*contentio*), paronomasia (*annominatio*), the use of more than one metaphor for the same referent (*frequentatio*), various kinds of verbal repetition (*expolitio, interpretatio*), and others. Such lore was ubiquitous in medieval education.

But there is little point in further documenting the obvious:

> Indeed, it would seem that any writer employing language which departs from strict subject-predicate order would be liable to a charge of using 'coloured' language. . . . The basic problem is that Roman rhetoricians and grammarians managed to account for almost every possible use of language. Their taxonomy was transmitted into the Middle Ages by Donatus, *ad Herennium*, and the encyclopedists, with the result that a man like Vinsauf could list more figures than any writer could avoid using.[14]

Even to prove that the English poets had all implemented the teachings of every Latin grammar book and treatise on rhetoric, *praedica-*

toria and *versificatoria*, would prove nothing to the point. For rhetorical devices have meaning only in context. In order to understand them, one must understand the full intention of the poem in which they occur and which they, in part, comprise. They exist, then, for the sake of the poem and not vice versa. But there is no need to apologize for studying Middle English short poems. They have unique priority in the history of the English lyric: they come first. Except for C. S. Lewis, hardly any modern poets use true Anglo-Saxon meters; but in spite of the vast predominance of free verse in various states of freedom, the Middle English tradition of rhymed, accentual-syllabic verse, sometimes even logical in structure, remains alive. It is to the continuance of that tradition that this study is dedicated.

2. Public, Practical, Anonymous

nlike their modern counterparts, most short poems from the English Middle Ages derive their meaning from large cultural values or institutions. They are <u>social artifacts</u>, <u>public and useful</u>, whose purpose can be gauged only with respect to a larger purpose. They represent, in short, the logical opposite of *l'art pour l'art*, the doctrine that "all art is quite useless."[1]

Poets and Audiences

As one might expect, the greatest repository of practical-poetic values was the medieval church, which touched the social as well as the intellectual life of the people at every point. One might, indeed, regard most of the poets as self-effacing workers who dedicated their art to the service of the church, just as the medieval masons worked together to build cathedrals. John Ruskin's estimate of the cathedral-builders applies very well, in fact, to those who labored on the immaterial fabric of the church.[2] The masons and the poets were both artisans, and both are essentially anonymous.

These poets were clergymen (friars, monks, and secular priests), minstrels, members of the upper middle class or nobility, and professional writers connected with a scriptorium or some other supporting institution; their poems, mainly religious in theme and purpose, were meant to be read in private, sung, or recited. Probably most of the clerical poets were friars, usually Franciscans, who, with the Dominicans, accounted for five of the six large commonplace books or miscellanies that survive from the thirteenth century. The sixth and best known miscellany is Harley 2253, copied piecemeal by monks at a religious house in Leominster, but containing a good many lyrics by friars.[3] We must imagine the Harley manuscript, and others like it, coming slowly into existence as different monks and friars copied down poems from recitation, probably at entertainments after supper.[4] The modern reader may be surprised to find that clerical recreation, which involved such fully secular items as "Alysoun" from the Harley manu-

11

script, did not include Christmas carols. This is because most of the carols were apparently meant to be sung in church processions, not to provide worldly entertainment.[5] Nearly all the carols are ecclesiastical in theme, and many were written by Franciscans, who sometimes used them in preaching.[6] And other kinds of poems were used in preaching; they can be found in collections of Latin sermons and sermon materials, such as the Franciscan *Fasciculus Morum* or the commonplace book (1372) of John Grimestone, a Franciscan friar. Any preacher, friar or secular, could use English verse mnemonically to impress a point on his congregation or to remind himself of what he meant to say. Finally, a clerk might compose hymns, or translate them from Latin, not only for preaching but also for the private devotions of upper-class laymen, who often entered such verses into their prayer books or Latin *Horae*, sometimes including specific, practical directions: "This praer here folwyng schold be sayd bifore the leuacion dewouteli kneling."[7]

It seems that these upper-class laymen, at least the merchant class of fifteenth-century London, really had very little interest in books, even though literacy was fairly widespread.[8] To the extent that they prized books for more than their cash value, they preferred devotional and liturgical writings. But some of them, like some of the clergy, entrusted bits of verse and favorite proverbs to flyleaves (our major sources for popular verse, which was often considered too trivial to preserve otherwise). And we do find rare individuals like Humfrey Newton (1466–1536), who not only copied down verses by Lydgate and others but even composed seventeen mediocre poems himself.

The other main class of laymen who copied and composed lyrics were the professional scriveners, who were well established in England by the thirteenth and fourteenth centuries;[9] by the fifteenth century, there was a large enough middle-class public to support a man like John Shirley (d. 1456), whose scriptorium turned out most of the expensive Aureate Collections.[10] But the brutal, prolonged War of the Roses, which lasted from 1455 to 1485, removed the demand for these luxury items by removing most of the English nobility; after this period, formal dedications vanish from the anonymous shorter works that continued to be written.[11]

The third group of lay poets, the minstrels, are the most obscure social class, though they seem the most familiar to modern imaginations. We cannot associate names with any particular poems, nor can we be absolutely sure they wrote any of the poems that have come down to us. We presume, from the size and contents of three so-called minstrel collections (e.g., Sloan MS. 2593), that they were indeed written by minstrels: all are pocket-sized (about 6 by 4½ inches), and they contain obvious folk songs like "Jolly Jankyn" (p. 122), though most of the songs and carols are religious. The presumptive evidence is, however, good enough; we need not imagine clerics, merchants, or scriveners singing "we bern abowtyn non cattes skynnys" (p. 106).

Intentions

If we analyze the uses and intentions of the Middle English poems, we can distinguish—in theory, at least—three irreducible motives, two of them social and one intellectual.* All three may serve religious or purely secular ends. The social impulses are to *celebrate*, usually with reference to an actual feast, and to *persuade*, with reference to specific actions. Persuasion here includes praying, cursing, and merely wishing. The third impulse, more intellectual than social, is to *define* a more or less widely accepted position or doctrine. The three motives are practical and dynamic; they are concerned with affecting people's lives, either directly or by a kind of intellectual conversion. The poems are not meant to be "things of beauty [and] joys forever," valuable in themselves. Their functional nature is more obvious if we remember that poems were written or otherwise used in various public places; they were "embroidered into tapestries, [used in] sotelties for elaborate dishes of food, tables to be exhibited in churches as aids for religious or political orientation, *tituli* for stained glass windows, posies for rings, and of course inscriptions for monumental brasses and tombs."[12]

Every poem must be understood as spoken from a point of view: the poet himself, or an absolute authority, or some persona is speaking the lines. The points of view behind these anonymous poems are, of course, vehicles for their intentions; thus a poet may address us from the standpoint of a dying sinner, in order to make us repent. The following provide typical points of view: Everyman (perhaps the most important), a minstrel, a drinker or reveler, Christ, a courtly or not-

---

* I am referring, here and throughout, only to original intentions and purposes, as distinct from the various uses to which the poems may conceivably be put (therapeutic, historical, purely aesthetic, and so on).

so-courtly lover, a dying sinner. Each of these in turn may be classified according to its cultural basis or source, most of which are, as I have said, associated with the church.

One very common basis for points of view is not, however, necessarily religious: the speaker of a poem may be defined by his social function or position, taken in a sense broad enough to include revelers, minstrels, an abused schoolboy, or a book-owner. The second main source is Scripture or religious doctrine, which informs the poems written from the standpoint of Christ or the Virgin Mary. A third important basis for points of view is nonreligious doctrine or theory. Thus, the many forlorn or hopeful lovers depend for words and sentiments on the elaborate "art of courtly love";* and the antifeminist derives his bitter attitudes from very old and popular lore with excellent scholarly credentials. Finally, a religious or existential† position may determine the writer's point of view, as in poems spoken by Everyman, a dying sinner, or a penitent monk-to-be. But whatever the cultural basis, medieval poetic intentions, always practical, are mediated by publicly accessible points of view, not by private personae, in order to affect behavior.

CELEBRATION: Most of the poems are occasional, in the sense that their full meaning can be understood only with regard to a specific social occasion. This is especially and obviously true of the festive poems (drinking songs, Christmas carols, and the like).[13] To understand these poems as well as possible, the modern reader must use his historical imagination. For not only is the accompanying music lost, in most cases, but the entire social setting of the poems has disappeared, except for a few faded vestiges here and there. To read medieval feast songs in one's study is like reading parts of the Latin mass at home, instead of going to the cathedral on Christmas Eve. But cathedrals are still available, and manorial banquet halls are not.

At best, then, we should fortify ourselves with history. Not with the necessarily abstract products of modern scholarship, but with actual documents from the Middle Ages, trivial and profound alike.[14]

---

* I am referring to the complex of feelings and ideas which Andreas Capellanus portrayed in *De arte honesti amandi*—not to the book itself.

† By existential I mean "pertaining directly to existence" rather than to doctrines, ideas, and institutions. An existential position is, for example, one's age or state of health.

14

Only thus can we hope to build up a store of associations, so that the simplest drinking song will reverberate with historical meaning. But since much detailed antiquarianism of this kind would be digressive here, I will content myself with a few facts about large-scale medieval feasting, followed by descriptions drawn from a fourteenth-century romance.

The manorial Christmas feast was above all exuberant, even gargantuan, partly because the preceding Advent fast had been so severe[15] and partly for economic reasons: the farm animals had just been slaughtered, the harvest was in, and the peasants had no pressing work to do in the fields. So the lord of the manor feasted his tenants on Christmas Day, supplementing the seasonal abundance of food with great quantities of beer and wine. The peasants also had to bring gifts of food, but the twelve work-free days of Christmas must have compensated for this. And the lord's hall was not the only scene of festivity. In spite of opposition from the upper clergy, church naves were sometimes used for banquets, and the bishops themselves entertained sumptuously. For instance, "[Bishop] Walter Gray entertained the kings of England and Scotland to a banquet at York at Christmas 1252 which cost him over £2500,"[16] and "six thousand guests are said to have come to the feast of the aristocratic George Neville at his installation as Archbishop of York in 1467."[17]

Weddings and Easters[18] could also be lavish occasions, but Christmas in the great hall was pre-eminent. We can imagine upper-class medieval festivities best with the help of contemporary pictures, such as we find in the "Très riches heures" of the Duc de Berry; but in lieu of this, we would do well to see through the eyes of a very gifted fourteenth-century poet, the anonymous author of *Sir Gawain and the Green Knight*. This romance, done with unusually vivid, lovely details, begins with a description of Christmas celebrations at Camelot, based, of course, on courtly ideals and realities of the fourteenth century. A typical manor hall of this period was something like a college at Oxford or Cambridge. It was long and rectangular, with a dais or high table at one end for the host and his distinguished guests; for the less distinguished guests, there were long trestle tables at right angles to the dais, filling the hall. Opposite the dais was a screen with doors to a passageway that led, in turn, to the kitchen, pantry, buttery, and main entrance; above the screen was a minstrel gallery. The enormous hearth might be in the center of the hall or built into the side; the air was smoky, and the stone floor was covered with new rushes for the occasion. Dogs were abundant. I will translate or paraphrase from lines 36 to 129 of *Sir Gawain and the Green Knight*,[19] omitting here and there to make the account more typical, and aiming only at clear, slightly archaic prose:

> This king lay at Camelot upon Christmas, along with many a gracious lord, men of the best, all the noble and courteous brethren of the Round Table, with fine reveling and carefree mirth. After many gay tourneys and jousts, these excellent knights went to the court to sing and dance at carols. For there the feast was a full fifteen days, with all the food and mirth that men could devise; such bright noises of merriment were glorious to hear, with sounds of merrymaking by day and dancing by night. All was happiness of the highest sort in halls and chambers, with lords and ladies doing what seemed to them of most delight. . . . As New Year had just arrived so freshly, the company on the dais were served that day a double portion, after the king had come with knights into the hall, and the chanting of mass had come to an end in the chapel. Loud cries were uttered by clerks and others there, 'Nowel' was repeated anew, called out full often. And then the young nobles ran forth to give out presents, loudly crying their New Year gifts, gave them in person, and busily debated over what was given [probably kisses]—ladies laughed full loud, though they had lost, and he that won was not angered, as you may well believe. All this mirth they made at dinner time. When they had suitably washed they went to their seats, the best man always in a higher place, as it seemed best; Queen Guenever, full gay, was set in the middle, arrayed on the splendid dais, adorned all about . . . . Bishop Bawdewyn was on King Arthur's right, and Ywain, Urien's son, ate beside the bishop. All these were placed on the dais and served magnificently, and afterwards many a trusty knight at the lower tables. Then the first course came with a sudden blasting of trumpets, and on the trumpets were hanging many a banner full bright; there was fresh noise of kettledrums with the noble pipes—wild, shrill, quavering notes and loud-wakened echoes—that many a heart rose high at their bursts of sound. Therewith came dainties made of full costly foods, an abundance of fresh meats, and on so many dishes that it was hard to find room in front of the people, to set on the tablecloth the silver vessels holding the various kinds of broth. Each knight, ungrudged, took for himself whatever he wanted. Every two people had twelve dishes, with good beer and bright wine both.

Such was the setting and atmosphere of a full-scale aristocratic feast in the Middle Ages, slightly idealized by the poet's omissions (there are no dogs fighting for scraps under the tables, and none of the peasants one would expect to find at Christmas open-house). Normally, the minstrel entertainment of songs and tales would follow the dinner and last an hour or two, perhaps with everyone seated on cushions around the fire. Secular entertainment of this kind was quite appropriate for weddings, coronations, and major religious festivals, which were therefore popular festivals as well; but at most castles and manors, no religious excuse was needed for listening to a jongleur.

To the religious and popular festivals, in a narrower sense, belong respectively the religious Christmas carols and the drinking songs, the one concerned with the gospel narrative and the other with sheer conviviality. But the carols were sung during lavish feasts, as at Camelot, and a drinking song could begin with a passage from St. John's Gospel:

	Verbum caro factum est	*The Word was made flesh*
	Et habitauit in nobis.	*And dwelt among us.*
	Fetys bel chere,	*Make good cheer*
4	Drynk to thi fere,°	*Companion*
	Verse le bauere,	*Pour out the drink*
	& synge nouwell![20]	

The intention of this poem and of the festive carols is thoroughly social, and for the most part there is no sharp distinction between speaker and audience. But it is not quite correct to speak of the *intention* of these poems, as if the poet were trying to tell us something about experience or doctrine. He does, to be sure, tell us things, but these facts and attitudes are only incidental. The Christmas carols and even the common drinking songs are communal poems of celebration; their cultural purpose is to celebrate the Good News or simply the state of being alive and healthy. This trilingual drinking song, for instance, tells us why we are celebrating ("Verbum caro"), and then delivers four imperatives that say essentially one thing: "celebrate!" But we learn nothing new; the biblical explanation is obvious, and imperatives, by their very nature, are not discursive.

In what sense, then, is celebration the purpose of this song? As I have suggested, the answer lies in understanding how the song fits into the feast as a whole. The purpose of the feast is to celebrate Christmas; the participants enjoy themselves, physically, because

Christ is born. The impulse to celebrate upon hearing that mankind is saved is, I trust, irreducible and axiomatic, just as the desire for good health is axiomatic.[21] The song, therefore, can be said to celebrate insofar as it contributes to the overall purpose of the feast, to which it is wholly subordinate. We must interpret the drinking song with respect to the acts of drinking and feasting, as we refer the meaning of a hand to the arm and body of which it is part.

There is no need to assume an elaborate feast as background for this song; no more of a feast is required than the convivial drinking that the song recommends. But if the words are incomplete without the music, drinking, eating, laughter, and the rest, is the converse true? What does the poem contribute to the feast? I believe that the answer can best be approached through analogies.

One of the functions of ritual language is to make us conscious of what we are doing, or what is being done to us, and thus complete the experience. A priest could bless his congregation simply by making the sign of the cross; everyone would understand the gesture, and the omitted words (". . . in nomine patris, filii, et spiritus sancti") would not have added any information or insights. But by including the words, an essential part of the *opus operatum*, the priest also renders the meaning of his gesture explicit, thus making the people's response more precise, ordered, and conscious. Even if the congregation did not understand Latin, merely to hear the words pronounced would lend formality to the gesture and encourage the listeners to pay attention.

Similarly, anyone who enjoys good food and drink knows that words can greatly concentrate his pleasure. Consider two opposite ways of drinking excellent wine: we may drink it down absent-mindedly, perhaps distracted by conversation, or we may think to ourselves, "I am drinking *Châteauneuf-du-pape* '61." And with the words would come associations. By using words, we bring to mind the full implications of what we are doing; we tell ourselves to pay attention.

This, I believe, is the main function of every song or poem meant to accompany a feast. A simple drinking song like "Verbum caro factum est" may support nothing more than the act of drinking communally, although this "simple" song happens to complicate the experience by including lines from the gospel of John. Other festive poems, such as the famous boar's head carol, are meant to be addressed

18

by a minstrel or master of ceremonies to the company of revelers; the purpose of these poems is to enhance the total sense of spectacle and festivity:

Caput apri Refero,	*I bring back the boar's head,*
Resonens laudes domino.	*Sounding praises to the Lord*
The boris hed In hondes I brynge,	
with garlondes gay & byrdes syngynge!	
I pray you all helpe me to synge,	
4 *Qui estis in conviuio.*	*Who are at this feast*
The boris hede, I vnderstond,	
ys cheff seruyce° in all this londe,	*course*
wher-so-ever it may be fonde,	
8 *Seruitur cum sinapio.*	*It is served with mustard*
The boris hede, I dare well say,	
anon after the XIIth day,	
he taketh his leve & goth a-way—	
12 *Exiuit tunc de patria.*	*Then he has gone from the country*

The refrain directs the attention of the group to the actual boar's head, and to the procession of revelers coming into the hall; the burden and first stanza refer to the activity of the moment, the spectacle and procession in which all are engaged; and the second and third stanzas do honor to the boar's head, the symbol of Christmas feasting, by listing some of its chief properties. Both "Verbum caro" and the boar's head carol and, indeed, the whole genre of "festive poem," are thus radically denotative: the words are perfectly subordinate to what they denote; they efface themselves in the presence of the persons, things, and actions to which they refer. Their essential message is "pay attention."

With some reservations, the same analysis can be applied to the more strictly religious poems of festivity. The Christmas carol beginning "Salvator mundi, domine" is strongly devotional and theological, with firm roots in the New Testament; and each stanza begins with a line from a Latin hymn found in the Sarum and the York breviaries.[22] Yet in spite of all these accoutrements, the real purpose of the carol is neither devotional nor didactic but festive. It is a full and obvious statement—at least in outline—of the meaning of Christmas, from the standpoint of all Christian revelers singing to each other, "make ye mery, for hym þat ys ycom" (line 11). The fourth stanza, especially,

reveals the occasion which the carol serves: a communal celebration of
the Nativity, with music if not food and drink. The first three stanzas,
largely devotional in content, fasten our attention on particular things
to be remembered and even savored—the Annunciation, God's loving
gift of his son—much as the boar's head carol stresses the boar's head
and the procession, or "Verbum caro" makes us think about our convivial drinking. In all three cases, the poem makes us pay attention to
particular aspects or implications of what we are doing in company:

> Alleluya Alleluya deo patri sit gloria[1]
>
> | | |
> |---|---|
> | Saluator mundi, domine, | *Savior of the world, Lord* |
> | ffader of heuene, yblessyd þu be! | |
> | þu gretyst A mayde with one° Aue, | *an* |
> | 4   *Alleluya, Alleluya!* | |
>
> | | |
> |---|---|
> | Ad-esto nunc propicius, | *Come now closer* |
> | þu sendyst þy sonne, swete Iesus, | |
> | Man to be-cum for loue of vs, | |
> | 8   *Alleluya deo!* | |
>
> | | |
> |---|---|
> | Te reformator sensuum, | *Thou reformer of (our) senses* |
> | lytyll & mekell,° All & some, | *great* |
> | make ye mery, for hym þat ys ycom, | |
> | 12   *Alleluya deo!* | |
>
> | | |
> |---|---|
> | Gloria tibi, domine, | *Glory be to thee, Lord* |
> | Ioy & blysse A-monge vs be! | |
> | ffor Att thys tyme borne ys he, | |
> | 16   *[Alleluya, Alleluya!]* | |

These three poems, and medieval festive poems in general, differ
sharply from their closest modern equivalents. "The Symposium," by
J. V. Cunningham, will serve as an example:

> Over the heady wine,
> Well-watered with good sense,
> Come, sing the simple line
> 4 And charm confusion hence.
>
> The fathers on the shelves
> Surely approve our toasts,

[1] *Alleluia, Alleluia, glory be to God the Father*

20

Surely are here themselves,
8   Warm, amiable ghosts,

Glad to escape the new
Regenerate elect
Who take the social view
12   And zealously reject

The classic indignation,
The sullen clarity
Of passions in their station,
16   Moved by propriety.[23]

This poem clearly makes use of the drinking song convention; that is, the poet expects us to imagine the lines being read at a convivial gathering of humanists. But "humanist" is the key word, not "convivial gathering." The real interest of the poem lies in its praise of certain values associated with Renaissance humanism, and its condemnation of certain modern values: "good sense" and the "simple line" are opposed to "confusion," and the whole fourth stanza is opposed to "the social view" of "the new/Regenerate elect." Only the first line refers merely to drinking; even the references in lines 5 through 7 are meant to assure us of moral support from the "amiable ghosts," not to draw our attention to the drinking. The verses are filled with connotations and innuendo, as befits an attempt to define a very personal and subtle complex of attitudes. The actual feast, the social occasion itself, is a mere device, not, as in the Middle Ages, the raison d'étre of the poem. It is this contrast between the public, practical, impersonal poetry of medieval England and the private, more thoughtful and subjective poetry of the modern period that I hope to illuminate, in all its stylistic ramifications, throughout this study.

PERSUASION: The second main public intention of the Middle English lyrics is to persuade. Like celebrating, persuasion is a social activity; but unlike the poems of celebration, those which intend to persuade are completely practical. The festive songs and carols are directly practical insofar as they contribute to the feast, but the feast itself is free, useless, and disinterested, in the Schillerian sense.[24] The poems of persuasion are practical because they are meant to influence behavior, in the narrow sense of specific actions or types of action. The poet wants other people, God, Mary, or Christ to do certain things. His art is more like modern advertising than like modern abstract painting.

The author of the famous thirteenth-century lyric "Alysoun," for instance, wants to overcome the resistance of his lady:

Bytuene mersh & aueril
when spray° biginniþ to springe,° — *twigs; grow*
þe lutel foul° haþ hire wyl — *bird*
4 on hyre lud° to synge. — *language*

Ich libbe in louelonginge
for semlokest° of alle þynge; — *the most seemly*
He° may me blisse bringe, — *She*
8 icham in hire baundoun.° — *power*
An hendy hap ichabbe yhent, — *I've had a fine stroke of luck*
ichot° from heuene it is me sent— — *I know*
from alle wymmen mi loue is lent,° — *gone*
12 & lyht° on Alysoun. — *(is) settled*

On heu° hire her is fayr ynoh, — *hue*
hire browe broune, hire eʒe blake,
Wiþ lossum° chere he on me loh°; — *lovely; smiled*
16 wiþ middel smal & wel ymake.
Bote° he me wolle to hire take — *Unless*
forte buen hire owen make, — *to be her own mate*
Longe to lyuen ichulle° forsake — *I shall*
20 & feye° fallen adoun. — *doomed*
An hendy hap &c.

Nihtes when y wende° & wake— — *turn (in bed)*
for-þi myn wonges waxeþ won— — *wherefore my cheeks wax wan*
leuedi, al for þine sake,
24 longinge is ylent° me on. — *fallen*
In world nis non so wyter° mon — *wise*
þat al hire bounte° telle con; — *bounty, excellence*
Hire swyre° is whittore þen þe swon, — *neck*
28 & feyrest may° in toune. — *maid*
An hendi &c.

Icham for wowyng al forwake, — *I am sleepless from wooing*
wery so water in wore, — *as weary as restless water (?)*
lest eny reue me my make — *lest anyone deprive me of my mate*
32 ychabbe y-ʒyrned ʒore. — *whom I have long yearned for*

Betere is þolien whyle sore[1]
þen mournen euermore;
geynest vnder gore,   *fairest under clothing*
36 Herkne to my roun.   *Listen to my song*
An hendi &c.

There are certainly other elements in the poem besides direct attempts at persuasion: the seasonal incipit, the praise of Alysoun, the intense longing; but all these can be subsumed under the intention to persuade. The two main themes of the poem—his praise of Alysoun (ll. 13–28) and his distress at not having her (ll. 5–8, 17–24, 29–35)—are the positive and negative sides of a single obvious strategy: to gain her favor by alternating flattery with threats. The poet states his intention explicitly, though in the third person: "Bote he me wolle to hire take / forte buen hire owen make, / Longe to lyuen ichulle forsake / & feye fallen adoun" (ll. 17–20). He concludes his plea even more directly, by addressing Alysoun: "geynest vnder gore, / Herkne to my roun" (ll. 35–36). The springtime incipit (ll. 1–4) establishes a hopeful, amorous mood in keeping with the poet's enterprise. Everything in the poem conspires to win Alysoun's love.

An even more clearly practical poem is the "Verses on a Chained Horae," which uses the same double-edged technique:

This present book legeble in scripture,°   *writing*
    Here in this place thus tacched° with a cheyn,   *attached*
Purposed of entent for to endure,
4   And here perpetuelli stylle to remeyne
    Fro eyre° to eyre; wherfore appone peyn   *heir (year?)*
        Of cryst-is curs, of faders and of moderes,
    Non of hem hens attempt it to dereyne,°   *remove*
8   Whille ani leef may goodeli hange with oder.° *other*

But for-as-moche that noo thyng may endure
    That urthely ys, alwey, y trowe, certeyn;
When-so-euer thys book here-aftyr in scripture
12 Eyder° in koueryng begynneth fause° ayeyn,   *or; give way*
    All tho therto that diligence doth or peyn
        Hit to reforme, be they on° or other,   *one*
    Haue they the pardon that criste yafe magdaleyn,
16   With daili blessyng of fader and of moder.

---

[1] *It's better to endure greatly for a while*

Gret reson wolde that euery creatur,
   Meued° of corage° on hit to rede or seyn,   *moved; spirit*
Shuld hym remembre in prayer that so sure
20   Bothe preeste and pace and bokes lust° ordeyn   *wished to*
    At his gret cost, John Harpur, noght to leyn°;   *conceal (his name)*
      Wherfor in speciall his eires wyth all oder
    Ar hyly bondon to pray the souereyn
24   Lord of all lordes present hym to hys moder.

The poem is meant to preserve the book on which it is inscribed, and to this end it offers a curse to anyone who might try to steal it (ll. 5–8) and a blessing to anyone who repairs it when necessary (ll. 9–16). The third stanza, a traditional request to pray for the book's owner, differs in specific purpose from the first two stanzas, though it is also meant to persuade. The opening lines stress the absolutely practical nature of the poem by referring to its precise circumstances, and by very clearly stating the purpose it serves. The first two lines rivet the poem to a specific place in present time; lines 3 to 5 explain what the poem is doing there, by stating a firm intention on behalf of the book and its owner. The book was indeed attached by a fifty-inch chain.[25] One can hardly imagine a more concretely useful poem.

    Others, such as the moral and didactic poems, are less concrete but no less practical. The brief epigram, "O man vnkynde," is penitential in purpose; it tells the listeners to repent and change their lives for the sake of Christ:

O man vnkynde°   *unkind, unnatural*
Haue thow yn mynde
My passyon smert   *My passion's suffering*
4 Thow shall me fynde
To the full kynde
Lo here my hert

And it does so with a variant on the strategy we have seen in "Alysoun" and the "Verses on a Chained Horae": Christ, speaking either from the cross or from eternity, first refers us to his suffering (ll. 1–3), then promises a reward for our good behavior (ll. 4–5). The last line, in which Christ appears to display his heart, as he does in the Corpus Christi drama and in much medieval iconography,[26] refers back to the passion theme and further underscores Christ's loving sacrifice for man. There is no explicit plea that we repay this love by exchanging vice for virtue, but the hint is unmistakable.

Although "O man vnkynde" puts words in the mouth of Christ, it was no doubt actually spoken by his representative, the priest, in order to convert the people. The numerous medieval prayers, on the contrary, were ostensibly spoken by the people to Christ (Mary, God) in order to "convert" him (them). Of course this analysis does not do justice to the logic of petitionary prayer, as we can see from a simple fourteenth-century example. "Mayde and moder mylde" asks the Virgin for help:

> Mayde and moder mylde,
> uor loue of þine childe
> þet is god an man,
> 4 Me þet am zuo wylde
> uram zenne þou me ssylde   *may thou shield me from sin*
> ase ich þe bydde can.   *as I (can) pray thee*
> Amen.

The suppliant's foremost desire is to be free of sin, but this is precisely what the penitential poems tell him: repent! The difference is in emphasis. The usual "repent!" poem stresses the sinner's own volition, whereas any prayer of supplication recognizes the need for grace; the process of conversion requires that divine grace and the sinner's free will both cooperate. But whether the penitent addresses himself or God, his purpose—to gain eternal life by improving his actual behavior—is directly practical.

Most poems in the *contemptus mundi* tradition are practical in the same penitential way. The tradition was very old, complex, and influential in European history;[27] but its origins concern us less than its immediate impact on thought and feeling in the late Middle Ages. If it is important to grasp the historical context of feast songs, it is just as important to understand the medieval setting of the *contemptus* poems, which make up a very large proportion of the moral-didactic lyrics in Middle English. In this area we have no charming romances to assist our historical imaginations; but there is much evidence from social history and the visual arts.

It is clear that the medieval Englishmen who recited and listened to *contemptus* poems had a much more intimate, vivid knowledge of death and suffering than we do. Infant mortality was very high, and

25

most people prepared and buried the dead with their own hands. Medical techniques were often fatal. Anesthetics had not been invented; the need for cleanliness was ill understood; and surgery might consist of massive bloodletting or summary amputation with an axe. Society was especially helpless in the face of epidemics, the worst of which was the Black Death. Most of us assume that nuclear war would be an unprecedented disaster; but there is a precedent. The Black Death spread northward through England from 1348 to 1350, killing a third or more of the population; and it recurred almost as badly in 1361, 1362, and 1369. This is nearly as if sixty or eighty million Americans were to die in two years as a result of germ warfare and its aftereffects. The Black Death would have been less crippling to medieval communities because they were rural, largely self-sufficient, and not highly specialized; but we cannot deny medieval Englishmen their palpable sense of death and decay, which they expressed so strongly in the preaching, writing, and art of the fourteenth and fifteenth centuries, and which at times overwhelmed their true penitential purpose.[28]

Thus the medieval preacher, especially the friar, would "point his audience to the skulls and bones of the departed, bidding them reflect how through the mouth once so delectable to kiss, so delicate in its eating, through eyes but a short while before so fair to see, worms now crawl in and out."[29] Paintings, woodcuts, and sculpture of the period, as well as the poems, embody the same themes and procedures. On the tomb of Jean Cardinal de Lagrange (d. 1402) in Avignon Cathedral, there is a stone effigy of the cardinal's body on its back, putrefying, with ribs and the sinews of neck and arms showing through the skin. Visitors to fifteenth-century English churches have noticed similar tomb sculpture, in which the bodies of dignitaries, male and female alike, are displayed in a state of maximum indignity, crammed with toads and worms, bloated or semidissolved. The very stone takes on some of the soft impermanence of flesh.

The English poetic branch of the *contemptus* tradition is, by contrast, relatively penitential, especially in the earlier part of the Middle English period; the poet usually remembers to moralize in some fashion. The *contemptus* poems are thus very similar in themes and purpose to certain products of English parochial Christianity. As R. W. Ackerman has shown, the various manuals of instruction for parish priests, such as Higden's *Speculum Curatorum* or Myrc's *Manuale Sacerdotale*, emphasized "the interrogation of the penitent as to his religious knowledge and . . . the administration of penance."[30] These tracts, which by the fourteenth century were extremely widespread and influential, included as part of the religious knowledge necessary to penitence many of the motifs, images, and the like, that also occur in the *vanitas* poems. The following observations on the Middle English *Desputisoun betwen þe Bodi and þe Soule* also apply, with few restrictions, to the short *contemptus* poems:

> . . . the *Desputisoun* may be shown to carry over from religious writings a series of images and formulations of a distinctly popular, vernacular cast that are alien to the Latin poems [predecessors of the Middle English poem]. These comprise allusions to the practice of witchcraft, to the world, the flesh, and the devil, to Matins, Mass, and Evensong, to false executors, to the need for confession, and to the hideousness of the rotting corpse. The importation of material of this sort obviously has an effect on the tone of the poem [p. 551] . . . In resorting to the very phraseology of parochial religion, the poet, responding to his basic sense of fitness, in all likelihood . . . prepared the way for his much more explicit [than in the Latin models] emphasis on the theme of the work: man's need for confession and amendment in this life.
>
> (Ackerman, pp. 551 and 564)

Only the reference to witchcraft, matins, mass, and evensong are unimportant in the short poems, which otherwise seem to be based as solidly as the *Desputisoun* on the teachings of parochial Christianity. A good though relatively genteel example is the fifteenth-century "Worldys blys, haue good day!" (p. 69), whose apparent purpose is to condemn, dramatically, the dying but unrepentant sinner's hopeless state of affairs. The actual purpose is penitential; the poet is telling us, "this is what it feels like to die in a state of mortal sin—therefore repent!" Among the more coarsely physical *contemptus* poems is "Wanne mine eyhnen misten" (p. 100), which still cannot equal tomb sculpture in vividness.

There are, then, many kinds of short poems that try directly or indirectly to persuade people to do certain things. Some are quite indirect, like "Wenest þu, huscher," in which a schoolboy threatens a sadistic usher who beats him daily:

27

Wenest þu, huscher, with þi coyntyse,[1]
Iche day beten us on þis wyse,[2]
  As þu wer lord of toun?
4 We had leuur scole for-sake,
  & ilche° of us an-oþur crafte take,   *each*
    þen long to be in þi bandoun.°   *power*

but wolde got þat we myth° ones   *might*
8 cache þe at þe mulne° stones,   *mill*
    or at þe crabbe tre—
  We schuld leue in þe such a probeyt°   *evidence*
  ffor þat° þu hast us don & seyd,   *that which*
12   þat alle þi kyn suld rwe° þe.   *pity*

&° þow sire robert,° with his cloke,   *if; (the devil)*
Wold þe helpe & be þi ppoke,°   *familiar spirit*
  þe were þu schust fare;   *the worse thou shouldst fare*
16 & for his prayer þe raþur° we wold *all the sooner*
  ʒyuen hym stripes al un-colde,
    not for hym þe spare.

ffor ofte sore we abye°   *pay for*
20 þe twynkelinges of his° hye,   *(the devil's eye)*
    þe maystur us to bete;[3]
  ffor he & þu are at asent,°   *in accord*
  Al day ʒyuen agagement°   *make an agreement*
24   to ʒyuen us strokes grete.

The schoolboy's implicit purpose is to change the usher's style of conduct. Others are direct, like the majority of prayers.* In any case, the poems of persuasion share with the festive lyrics a specifically social kind of usefulness.

DEFINITION: The third major intention is to define. It is a less directly social impulse than the other two, but still ultimately concerned with affecting behavior. Most such poems are religiously didactic: they define doctrines and moral states in order to Christianize

---

[1] *Dost thou think, usher, with thy cunning,*
[2] *To beat us each day in this manner*
[3] *(indicating that) the master beat us*

  * Songs and hymns of pure praise and devotion are rare; most are petitionary.

their audience, on the assumption that true conversion is more likely when a person understands the content of his religion. This is not to say that the poems of definition move on a high intellectual plane; they are not at all comparable in depth, precision, and thoroughness to the methods of St. Thomas Aquinas. Nor would such methods be appropriate, since the poems were aimed at the Christian Everyman of the Middle Ages, who was usually illiterate and unfamiliar with the fine logic of scholasticism. The poems are closer to devotional than to doctrinal writings; they attempt to convey the feelings motivated by what they define.

But the impulse to define was broad enough to include even love songs such as "Continvaunce / Of remembraunce," from the so-called Findern Anthology:

> Continvaunce
> Of remembraunce
>   withowte endying
> 4 Doth me penaunce
> And grete greuaunce
>   ffor your partynge.
>
> So depe ye be
> 8 Grauene, parde,°   *by God, indeed*
>   with-yn myn hert,
> That A-fore mee
> Euer I yow see,
> 12 In thought couert.°   *covert, hidden*
>
> Though I ne playn°   *complain about*
> My wofull payn
>   But bere yt styll,
> 16 It were in vayn
> To sey again   *to speak against*
>   ffortunes wyll.

This graceful courtly poem, so reminiscent of Wyatt's songs, defines the poet's grief by explaining it at some length. In the first stanza, he explains that the cause of his "penaunce / And grete greuaunce / for your partynge" is his "Continvaunce / Of remembraunce / withowte endying." The second stanza is more precise and graphic: "Continvaunce / Of remembraunce" really means that the poet continually sees his mistress in his mind's eye (ll. 10–12) because she is deeply engraved in his heart (ll. 7–9). The third stanza merely comments on the vanity of speaking against fortune. The poem thus succeeds in causally defining the lover's grief and, by implication, his loyalty.

Most poems of definition are, however, specifically religious. Among the Marian poems, the following is the shortest and probably the most definitive:

> In all this worlde ys none so tru,
> As she that bare our Lorde Jhesu.

This epigram defines the Virgin in two ways: by claiming that she is absolutely "tru" and by referring to her supreme function. The second, of course, guarantees the first. There is a strong suggestion that Mary will certainly reward her devotees, and there is praise for her; but the suggestion is a corollary, and the praise is part of the couplet's chief purpose: to explain exactly who the Virgin is.

Much the same technique is applied to define Christmas in "A songe to syng Y haue good ryght," one of the more theological carols:

> *Laus, honor, virtus, gloria,*[1]
> *Et tibi decus, Maria.*[2]
> *Laus, honor, virtus, gloria,*
> *Et tibi decus, Maria.*

> 1
> A songe to syng Y haue good ryght,
> And myrth to make in this presens,
> For now ys borne a baron of myght,
> *Mundum pugillo continens.*[3]

> 2
> This babe was borne on Youle nyght,
> In Bedlehem of Oure Lady;
> The name of hym is called ryght
> *Verbum Patris Altissimi.*[4]

> 3
> That nowe is come pees for to make
> Bytwene the Fader of Hevyn and vs;

[1] *Praise, honor, virtue, glory,*
[2] *And splendor be to thee, Maria.*
[3] *Holding the world in his fist.*
[4] *The word of the Highest Father.*

30

And nowe for that childys sake
   Exultet celum laudibus.[5]

4

Oure synne to slee he toke the way
   Into the worle fro heuyn riche blysse,[6]
And therfore bothe nyght and day
   Resultet terra gaudiis.[7]

5

The childe fellyd° alle the fendys pride   *felled*
   And with harde yren bonde hym in cloos,
And with the blode of his dere syde
   Soluit a pena miseros.[8]

6

Nowe Jhesu Cryst, that come so stylle
   Into the wombe of Mary fre,°   *Noble*
We praye the, yyf hit be thy wylle,
   Mane nobiscum, Domine.   *Remain with us, Lord*

The first and fourth stanzas explain why singing and "myrth" are appropriate at Christmas, and the bulk of the carol supports this explanation by referring to the Christmas story in Stanza 2 and to doctrinal interpretations of Christ's career in Stanzas 2 to 5. The final stanza, a traditional closing prayer, continues to define Christ in the same operational way that "In all this worlde" defines his mother, and in language reminiscent of the famous "I syng of a myden" (p. 83). Although the carol is also celebratory, it celebrates by defining the rationale for Christmas joy.

All three intentions—to celebrate, persuade, and define—are irreducible in that they cannot be theoretically resolved into each other or into even more fundamental motives. They may, however, qualify each other in practice: a poem may persuade by defining, or define while incidentally persuading, or persuade someone to celebrate by defining the feast. The possibilities are many, if not endless. But in most poems, one of these three practical intentions clearly predominates.

---

[5] *May heaven rejoice with praises.*
[6] *From the bliss of the kingdom of heaven*
[7] *May the earth resound with joys.*
[8] *Released from pain those who were suffering.*

General Sources for Points of View

These three intentions, like all intentions realized in words, are mediated by points of view rooted in the contemporary culture. If, for example, the speaker of a fourteenth-century poem is Jesus Christ, we must consult the New Testament, preferably the Latin version known to the Middle Ages, and contemporary medieval traditions both popular and academic, in order to find out exactly who this medieval Jesus Christ is. Similarly, if the speaker of the poem is a courtly lover, we must become familiar with the doctrines of courtly love, as defined —say—by Andreas Capellanus, in order to fully understand this point of view. The poem, in other words, presupposes a knowledge of certain sources that explain its point of view. Thus the New Testament and tradition, and the doctrine of courtly love, are what I would call the general sources for Christ and the courtly lover as literary points of view.

I believe that a handful of general sources account for the points of view of most Middle English poems. These sources are truly general in the sense of being "publicly accessible" and "referring to large classes of common things," as contrasted with the usual source for modern points of view, the poet's intimate self-awareness. The medieval sources are the following: social role or position, Scripture or religious doctrine, nonreligious doctrine or theory, and broadly religious or existential positions. All of these support points of view which are general and public, not unique like modern products of introspection.

The point of view in a festive song or carol is usually defined by the speaker's social function or status: "Verbum caro" is spoken by a reveler, and "The boris hed" by the leader of the procession. Both speakers are defined by their temporary role in a social event—a feast or a drinking bout. The same is true of the following Christmas carol:

> Proface,° welcom, wellcome.   [a greeting]
> This tyme ys born a chylde of grace,
> That for vs mankynde hathe take,
>   Proface.
> This day is born a childe of grace,
> That for vs mankynde hathe take,
>   Proface.

1

A kynges sone and an emperoure
Ys comyn oute of a maydynys toure,
With vs to dwelle with grete honowre,
    Proface.

2

This holy tyme of Cristesmesse
All sorwe and synne we shulde relese
And caste away all heuynesse,
    Proface.

3

The gode lord of this place entere°   *entire*
Seith welcome to all that now apere
Vnto suche fare as ye fynde here,
    Proface.

4

Wellcome be this New Ere,
And loke ye all be of gode chere.
Oure Lorde God be at oure denere!
    Proface.

The speaker welcomes the revelers to the dinner on behalf of "the gode lord of this place entere." All such carols define their points of view in relation to the needs of the feast; as a result, any number of individuals can fit into the speaker's role.

But generality of this sort does not completely exclude personal qualities:

D . . . dronken—
    dronken, dronken y-dronken—
. . . dronken is tabart atte wyne.
4 hay . . . suster, walter, peter,
    ȝe dronke al depe,
    ant ichulle eke!   *and I shall too*
    stondet alle stille—
8   stille, stille, stille—
    stondet alle stille—
    stille as any ston;
    trippe a lutel wit þi fot,
12   ant let þi body go!

The speaker of the poem is a man in the act of drinking and probably dancing (the heavy, regular meter, and successive allusions to pausing in lines 7 through 10 and movement in lines 11 and 12 suggest a dance),[31] but even though his point of view exists with reference to a group activity, he is still able in lines 4 through 6 to cry out as an individual. Such personal, even biographical, details are rare in medieval poetry; no one could speak these lines *in propria persona* who did not have a sister, and friends named Walter and Peter. Still, the medieval principle of general applicability is not far to seek: one need only substitute the appropriate words for "suster, walter, peter," and anyone at all could speak the lines.

Among the other social institutions that supported points of view in the lyrics were the medieval school system and medieval book-ownership. The first made the song of a complaining schoolboy (p. 28) possible, and the second explains the need for "Verses on a Chained Horae" (p. 23). The speaker of the ominous carol "Anoder ȝere hit may betyde" appears to be a person of some importance in the manorial hall (ll. 5–7), whose point of view consequently implies the whole hierarchic social order of late medieval England:

Who wot° nowe þat ys here,	*knows*
Where he schall be anoder yere?	
Anoder ȝere hit may betyde	
Þis compeny to be full wyde,	
And neuer on-odyr to abyde;	
4 Criste may send now sych a ȝere.	
Anoþer ȝere hit may befall	
Þe lest° þat is withyn this hall	*least, lowest*
To be more mastur þen we all;	
8 Cryste may send now sych a ȝere.	
This lordis that ben wonder grete,	
They threton powre men for to bete;	
Hyt lendith° lytull in hur threte;	*There abides, is*
12 Cryste may send sich a yere.	

He defines himself with reference to those above and below him on the social scale. Like the festive basis for drinking songs and carols, these three sources could be analyzed sociologically.

Other sources must be approached mainly through philology. Pre-eminent among these are Scripture and religious doctrine, which underlie all poems written from the standpoint of Christ, the Virgin Mary, or any other biblical personage. Such poems are obviously not exercises in historical imagination, in which the poet tries to efface himself by empathizing with someone from the past; they are not even Yeatsian "masks" through which the poet speaks his own thoughts. Medieval quasi-dramatic poems may be best understood by comparison with modern poems in which the sense of a unique speaking voice is a major requirement. Browning's dramatic monologues represent one kind of "passionate, normal speech,"[32] as does much of Yeats, Eliot, and Pound. For instance, most of the memorable poems in Pound's early volume, significantly called *Personae*, are either translations or dramatic monologues spoken through some historical persona:

> 38 God! she was white then, splendid as some tomb
>   High wrought of marble, and the panting breath
> 40 Ceased utterly. Well, then I waited, drew,
>   Half-sheathed, then naked from its saffron sheath
> 42 Drew full this dagger that doth tremble here.
>   (from "Piere Vidal Old"[33])

The intention is obviously to create the effect of a real man speaking, especially in the phrasing of lines 38 and 40, and in the repetitions in the last three lines; the poet's own personality and intention are discernible only through the "mask," at second hand.

In the medieval "dramatic" poems, however, the point of view is ultimately homiletic; one hears the preacher quite distinctly through the thin mask of Jesus. And yet the mask is accurately modeled, as far as it goes, on Scripture and doctrine strongly colored by the new, intense devotion of Anselm, Bernard, Francis, and their followers. Bernard says in one of his sermons that "this was . . . the principal cause why the invisible God wished to be seen in the flesh and to converse with men, that he might draw all the affections of carnal men, who were unable to love except after the flesh, to the saving love of His flesh, and so step by step lead them to spiritual love."[34] Saint Francis, above all, brought to the medieval Everyman this ardent, personal devotion that concentrated on the physical humanity of Christ and the Virgin,[35] dwelling especially on the agonies of the cross and the tenderness of the nativity.[36] Thus the scriptural persona in medieval quasi-dramatic lyrics had graphic, palpable content; we cannot ignore it and merely say that the preacher is speaking, as usual, in favor of repentance. Insofar as the church represents Christ, we could in fact reverse this proposition and claim that all versified homilies are spoken by Christ through his preachers. Be that as it may, we can see the extent to which doctrine and Scripture define the speaker in the fourteenth-century "I am iesu, þat cum to fith":

> I am iesu, þat cum to fith°   *fight*
> With-outen seld° & spere,   *shield*
> Elles were þi det° i-dith°   *death; accomplished*
> 4 ȝif mi fithting ne were.
>
> Siþen i am comen & haue þe broth°   *brought*
> A blisful bote° of bale,   *remedy*
> Vndo þin herte, tel me þi þouth,°   *thought*
> 8 þi sennes grete an smale.

The figure of Jesus as the knightly champion of man is literary and traditional;[37] but the basis for this trope is in Scripture, where Jesus is the paradoxically helpless ("With-outen seld & spere") Son of God who dies to save mankind. In the second half of the epigram (ll. 5–8), Jesus speaks as a confessor, a persona based on traditional theories and practices devised much later than the time of Christ's life on earth. Both aspects of the poem's speaker thus derive from publicly available sources.

One of the most striking poems in Middle English also derives its point of view, hence its authority, from Scripture and doctrine:

> I haue laborede sore and suffered deyȝth,
> and now I Rest and draw my breyght;
> but I schall come and call Ryght sone
> 4 heuene and erght and hell to dome;
> and thane schall know both devyll and mane,
> What I was and what I ame.

This poem is based on eschatological doctrine, and may perhaps be regarded as a dramatic comment on the credal *descendit ad inferos*. Its point of view is that of Christ speaking sometime between the crucifixion and doomsday. To have Christ speak under any circumstances is impressive enough; but to have him speak from an eschatological state, in such spare, quiet language, is awesome. The final line reverberates with the full power of its meaning, an implied answer to the most essential question of all: who is Christ?

Secular doctrine defines the speaker of most courtly love lyrics and of a few other poetic types, like the antifeminine satire. The pining lover of "Alysoun" (p. 22), for example, can be looked up in the textbooks on courtly love. He lives "in loue longinge" (l. 5), he is "in hire bandoun" (l. 8), he will die if she does not accept him (ll. 17–20), and, not least, he is losing a good deal of sleep on her account (ll. 22–24, 29–32). All of this is described in Andreas Capellanus and in many, many other poems.[38] But the very commonplaceness of "Alysoun," far from being a defect, is the essence of its original value: it could be used by any number of young men in the same general situation. They needed only to replace "Alysoun" with the appropriate name. The poem is an artifact for general use, in the sense that a bottle opener is meant for more than one bottle.

Antifeminine ideology is behind the soothsayer's response to a housewife's question in the lively little dialogue "Sey, wist y þe brom":

"Sey, wist y þe brom,	*Tell me, man in the broom (brush),*
þwat ys me for to don?	*what am I to do?*
Ich haue þe werreste bonde°	*husband*
4 þat ys in oni londe."	

responsio sortilege anglice	*the soothsayer's reply in English*
"þyf° þy bonde ys ylle	*If*
Held þy tonge stille."	

The final couplet clearly states the point of the epigram and its point of view. The garrulous housewife was a stock figure in the antifeminine literature that medieval churchmen so devoutly cultivated;[39] it is appropriate that one manuscript of the poem (Trinity College, Cambridge, Manuscript 323) was probably "compiled in a religious house, whose members entered into it from time to time material which they wished to preserve for their common use."[40] Antifeminine ideas were well articulated, authoritative, and certainly older than the doctrine of courtly love, which may have been equally widespread in the late Middle Ages.

Another general source for the speaker's point of view was his religious status or, even more broadly, his existential position. Unlike religious or secular doctrine, this category refers not to a set of ideas but to the speaker's locus in the medieval Christian life or in the natural life of common humanity. Thus a simple prayer like "[I]hū crist of Naȝareþ" is spoken by the Christian Everyman, a suppliant whose medievalness, aside from his language, shows only in his choice to pray by the five wounds as if he were swearing by them:

> *Oracio bona de ihū xⁱ*   *a good prayer of Jesus Christ*
> Ihū crist of Naȝareþ,
> > That for vs all suffriddist deþ
> > Vpon þe rode° tree,   *rood, cross*
> 4 Thorow vertu of ȝowre woundis v.
> > That ȝe suffryd in ȝoure lyue,
> > Haue mercy on me!
> > > Amen.

The immediate source for his point of view is not a complex doctrine of divine mercy, but his status as a Christian suppliant, as one who prays to Christ for mercy. Another, more limited Christian point of view is that of the penitent who resolves to become a friar:

> No more ne willi wiked be,
> Forsake ich wille þis world-is fe,°   *fee, reward*
> Þis wildis wedis,° þis folen° gle;   *clothes; fool's*
> 4 ich wul be mild of chere,
> of cnottis scal mi girdil be,
> becomen ich wil frere.°   *friar*
>
> Frer menur° i wil me make,   *Minorite (Franciscan)*
> 8 and lecherie i wille asake°;   *renounce*
> to ihesu crist ich wil me take
> and serue in holi churche,
> al in my ouris° for to wake,   *canonical hours*
> 12 goddis wille to wurche.
>
> Wurche i wille þis° workes gode,   *these*
> for him þat boyht° us in þe rode;   *bought*
> from his side ran þe blode,
> 16 so dere he gan vs bie—   *he bought us so dearly*
> for sothe i tel him mor þan wode¹   *who practices lechery*
> þat hantit licherie.

¹ *in truth I consider him more than crazy*

This persona is based on the facts of Christian sin and repentance and on the speaker's social position as a potential Minorite.

The basis for the existential point of view is even broader:

Þe leuedi° fortune is boþe frend and fo,   *lady*
Of pore che makit riche, of riche pore also,
Che turneȝ wo al into wele, and wele al into wo,
No triste° no man to þis wele, þe whel it turnet so.   *trust*

The speaker of an epigram such as this generalizes on experience from the standpoint of one who realizes that Lady Fortune, because she "turneȝ wo al into wele, and wele al into wo," cannot be trusted. The purpose of the epigram is to give moral advice, but the basis for its standpoint is common sense, which is not exclusively Christian and homiletic.

The general sources for medieval points of view are, then, public and open to inspection. They are accessible either to study, like Scripture and religious or nonreligious doctrines, or to personal experience and observation, like social function or position and religious or existential status. Although some of the poems, such as "Wenest þu, huscher," "D . . . dronken," or "No more ne willi wiked be," include personal details, these details can be replaced by others* to suit the particular speaker of the moment. A hallmark of the Middle English lyric is thus its impersonal, general applicability: it can be used by any one of a class of people (e.g., courtly lovers) for a general purpose (winning a lady). In this it contrasts abruptly with most modern poems.

The modern poet who best illustrates this contrast, and so helps define the medieval short poem, is probably G. M. Hopkins, who, although a priest in the nearest present-day equivalent of the medieval church, nonetheless concerned himself with personal uniqueness. The following is the octave from one of his late sonnets:

Not, I'll not, carrion comfort, Despair, not feast on thee;
Not untwist—slack they may be—these last strands of man
In me or, most weary, cry *I can no more*. I can;
Can something, hope, wish day come, not choose not to be.
But ah, but O thou terrible, why wouldst thou rude on me
Thy wring-world right foot rock? lay a lionlimb against me? scan
With darksome devouring eyes my bruised bones? and fan,
O in turns of tempest, me heaped there; me frantic to avoid thee and flee?[41]

---

* The place references in "Wenest þu, huscher" are a possible exception, since they are prominent and contribute to the tone of the poem.

The only source for this point of view, this "I," is Hopkins' self-awareness, born of tortured introspection and not publicly accessible. The poem's intention is to characterize the first-hand experience of one man—Hopkins; the contours of his language would not precisely fit anyone else, even a person very good at empathizing. Hopkins, the priest, has in fact defined, once and for all, this general source of so much modern poetry, in *Comments on the Spiritual Exercises of St. Ignatius Loyola:*

> Nothing else in nature comes near this unspeakable stress of pitch, distinctiveness, and selving, this selfbeing of my own. Nothing explains it or resembles it, except so far as this, that other men to themselves have the same feeling. . . . We say that any two things however unlike are in something like. This is the one exception: when I compare my self, my being-myself, with anything else whatever, all things alike, all in the same degree, rebuff me with blank unlikeness; so that my knowledge of it, which is so intense, is from itself alone, they in no way help me to understand it. And even those things with which I in some sort identify myself, as my country or family, and those things which I own and call mine, as my clothes and so on, all presuppose the stricter sense of *self* and *me* and *mine* and are from that derivative.[42]

But this is the voice of the modern world, speaking through a man steeped in medieval philsophy. The medieval poem, public and practical, is *essentially* anonymous; from this follows its whole stylistic nature.

3. Words and Metaphors

General Theory

n the sense that eighteenth-century descriptive verse seems heavily adjectival,[1] the dominant words in the Middle English poems are nouns, especially abstract nouns referring to moral, emotional, and existential reality, and what I shall call social nouns, referring to classes of people. This is what one might expect; in order to celebrate, persuade, or define, in the medieval English manner, a poem must relate a class of people (ladies, sinners, revelers, Christians, etc.) to a different kind of abstraction (love, sin, joy, death, heaven, etc.), or it may relate two abstractions such as sin and hell. The relationship itself is usually simple: the lady must *accept* the poet's love, the sinners must *avoid* sin and pursue virtue, revelers must *possess* joy, and, in poems of definition, one thing is usually shown to *be* another. The most prominent verbs, then, either denote a general movement of body or soul, often towards or away from something—seeking, avoiding, coming, going, loving, loathing, and so forth—or they establish bare relationship by means of the copula, the verbs of possession, or some other general connective. There are verbs denoting specific, vivid actions, but they do not set the tone of the Middle English lyrics.

When it appears, the world of concrete particulars is represented mainly by nouns, not by verbs or adjectives. These concrete nouns serve to modify the relationship between abstract and social nouns; they do not exist for their own sakes. Thus a plow and a cracked dish help describe a bad marriage (p. 78), and puddings, sauce, and rotten fish help define certain feelings about Advent (p. 76). If the intention of the poem is to persuade or define, the concrete nouns may be used figuratively, in some form of metaphor, paradox, or pun, to modify more sharply the primary relation between abstract and social nouns. (There are virtually no tropes in the poems of celebration.)

The intention of a poem is often modified in another way: its validity can be made absolute or comprehensive with proverbs and commonplaces or with expressions of magnitude, intensity, and the like. The poet may say that *everyone* should celebrate, or that his mistress is the *most* beautiful and virtuous of all, or that *no man* can escape death; and he sometimes gives his words authority by quoting proverbs and catch-phrases. It is clear, I think, that the poems lend themselves especially to this kind of intensifying because, to the extent that they are public, they should involve as many people as possible; and to the extent that they are practical, they should support their demands as strongly as possible.

To summarize, one can describe the generalized form of the poems —the shape of their inner logic, not their organization—in the following manner:

> An abstract noun is related [(figuratively) by a concrete noun]
> to a social noun or pronoun [and the relationship or either of its terms
> is modified by an intensifier].

For example,

> Howe cometh al ye That ben y-brought
> In bondes,—full of bitter besynesse
> of erthly luste, abydynge in your thought?
> 4   Here ys the reste of all your besynesse,
> Here ys the porte of peese, & resstfulness
> to them that stondeth In stormes of dys[e]se,
> only refuge to wreches In dystrese,
> 8 and all comforte of myschefe & mys[e]se.

In this poem the abstract noun is God, understood as "the reste of all your besynesse," "the porte of peese," and so forth;[2] the social pronoun is "ye," intensified by "al"; and the two terms are related by the conventional figure of man as the storm-tossed voyager with God his safe harbor and goal ("reste," "porte," "refuge," and "comforte"). The formula I have given does not take account of syntactic words, descriptive adjectives, or specific kinds of verbs; but it draws attention to the most important kinds of nouns, which are the chief loci of meaning in these strongly substantive poems.[3]

Abstract Nouns, Social Nouns, and Adjectives

In one sense, all common nouns are abstract because they refer to classes, not particulars; otherwise they would be unintelligible. Thus

42

an apparently concrete noun like *doorknob* refers to a general class of objects unless it is precisely qualified, as in "the glass doorknob on the inside of Mr. Eliot's front door," where the context ensures that we know which house is Mr. Eliot's, and so forth. Only by qualification can a common noun be truly concrete, in the sense of referring to one particular object or person.

In a narrower sense, however, a noun is abstract "if it is the name for a quality—'beauty,' 'brightness,' 'heat'—which cannot exist apart from the object or situation of which it is an attribute, or if it is the name for an entity—'poetry,' 'reason,' 'force'—which cannot be perceived."* It is mainly in this sense that I have defined one of the "chief loci of meaning" in the lyrics as an abstract noun. But this is not to imply that other nouns are truly concrete and vivid. I hope to show that nearly all medieval nouns, whether social or concrete or even personal, are essentially abstract because they are not strongly modified. Distinctions among abstract, social, concrete, and personal nouns are really distinctions among several kinds of abstraction that differ according to their referents. *Beauty, hangman,* and *cabbage* refer to different kinds of things.

Abstract nouns, then, are words for qualities and other intangibles. More specifically, abstract nouns in the short poems refer to moral, emotional, or existential realities; as a rule, they are not scientific or philosophical. The following† are some recurrent words for moral and emotional values: "gentyll chere," mirth, "gomen," sorrow, care, love, shame, courage, goodness, obedience, governance, repentance, vice, frailty (of the flesh), longing, pity, mercy, lechery, chastity, pride, sin, ingratitude, solace, worthiness, guilt, wrath, wrong, right, bliss, woe, and glee. Words for existential or supernatural values include: death, life, God, richness, poverty, weal, wretchedness, hell, heaven, plenitude, fortune, might, soul, strength, pain, naught, God's will, coming, having, and doom.

The second term in my general formula is the social noun. In the lyric, the significant social nouns classify people by their general function or position in society, not by very specific, ephemeral functions ("people who steal candlesticks from altars"). Some groups are de-

---

* M. H. Abrams, *A Glossary of Literary Terms* (New York, 1961), p. 1. Abrams will hereafter be cited in the text.
† When possible, I shall quote words in their modern forms.

fined morally or existentially (traitors, sinners, women, maidens, men, mankind, the dead, the strong, the young, the old), but much more typical are the following social classes: lords, messengers, butlers, ladies, "lemans," clerks, men (servants), fathers, kin, mothers, heirs, priests, queens, brothers, advocates, sisters, children, sons, friends, kings, neighbors, princesses, disciples, knights, squires, laboring men, monks, friars, canons, nuns, marshals, grooms, pages, and champions. Each of these words denotes a class of people because each is abstract in the sense that all common nouns are abstract. And each class is relatively broad; the poets do not speak of lutenists and bear-trainers.

Both the abstract and the social nouns, then, are general in meaning because they refer to qualities and ideas (love, sorrow, joy, sin) or to kinds of people (clerks, fathers, messengers). But their meanings are general for another reason: although the nouns are qualified to some extent by context, they receive very little specification from adjectives and adverbs, which in Middle English poems are usually quite broad in their range of meanings. The poets are content, by and large, simply to name the thing—from a boar's head to the love of God—rather than describe it vividly. A few passages, more adjectival than usual, will illustrate this tendency (italics mine):

My luff alone is one oone lente   *has alighted on one*
the whiche is *fayre, fecunde* and *fre,*°   *noble*
the *myldeste* may that euer was mente°   *spoken of*
        (15th:45)

Sent Iorge þat ys owre lady Knyȝte,
He tende þe tapyrys *fayre & Bryte*—
To myn yȝe a *semley* syȝte,
And By a chapell as y Came.
    Mery hyt ys.
        (15th:116)

þi loueliche handis loue haþ to-rent,°   *torn up*
And þi *liþe* arme[s] wel *streit*° itent;°   *tightly; stretched*
þi brest is *baar,* þi bodi is *bent,*
for wrong haþ wonne & riȝt is schent.
        (14th:90)

Go day, Syre Cristemas, our kyng,
For euery man, both *olde* and *yynge,*

Ys *glad* and *blithe* of your comynge;
   Go day!

(c:5)

The nouns themselves are general, as we might expect: one (a maiden), tapers, sight, hands, arms, breast, body, man, coming; and the adjectives do very little to make them specific and vivid. Many of the adjectives are subjective, in that they express the poet's broad approval rather than describing traits inherent in the object of his attention: fayre, fre, mildeste, semley, mery, loueliche. Of course this can be disputed on philosophical grounds; the poet might argue that his lady is inherently "fayre" and "fre," and that he has done nothing more than observe and name these qualities. To the post-Kantian modern reader, it does seem that the poet has applied his own categories to the lady; but the medieval poet could have been a realist bent on discovering *realia in rebus*. The adjectives "glad and blithe" are even more ambivalent. Are all the revelers actually "glad and blithe," in themselves, or does the poet merely say that they are?

But whether the adjectives are inherent or superimposed, they are quite nonspecific, as are the adjectives that refer more clearly to inherent traits, like fecunde, Bryte, liþe, streit, baar, bent, olde, and yynge. The formula "both olde and yynge" is meant to be comprehensive, not descriptive; "fecunde" does not distinguish the poet's lady from most other young women; and "Bryte" says nothing about the quality of brightness (shimmering, piercing, iridescent, etc.). The modifiers applied to Christ give a graphic outline of his body on the cross, but do not suggestively fill it in, except, perhaps, for "liþe" (supple, lithe).

Let us see how a modern poet uses adjectives to describe brightness, a quality that medieval aesthetics greatly prized:[4]

> Here luxury's the common lot. The light
> Lies on the rain-pocked rocks like yellow wool
> And around the rocks the soil is rusty bright
> From too much wealth of water, so that the grass
> Mashes under the foot, and all is full
> Of heat and juice and a heavy jammed excess.[5]

4

"Bright" (l. 3) modifies "soil," and is itself modified by "rusty" and "From too much wealth of water"; "soil" is also modified by its total context. In fact, just as every word in the stanza describes the soil di-

45

rectly or indirectly, so do all the nonsyntactic words modify each other. If English were an agglutinative language, the whole stanza could be a very complex word for a certain kind of soil: a soil which suggests that luxury's the common lot, which extends around rain-pocked rocks covered with light like yellow wool, and which is rusty bright from too much wealth of water, so that the grass mashes under foot . . . In this compound, the relationships are closely knit and unified because they are all concerned with a simple, restricted subject, a highly particular Provençal landscape. Therefore "soil," "bright," and all other such words, gain very precise meanings from the whole content.

One might perform the same analysis on the "tapyrys fayre & Bryte" of the second passage quoted, but the resulting complex would modify "tapyrys" in a different way: the agglutinative word would explain precisely who was tending the candles, how the poet happened to see them, and what he thought of them. This compound word for "tapyrys" would be moral* and circumstantial, not sensuous and vivid like the one for Richard Wilbur's soil. Thus "bright" is far more specific than the Middle English "Bryte"; it is modified not only by the adverb "rusty," but by a context that supports the sensuous quality of "bright" with further sensuous details, assonant and alliterative, whereas "Bryte" gets very little sensuous reinforcement from its context. As a result, both "Bryte" and "tapyrys" are less specific and more abstract than "bright" and "soil."

My essential point is that there are, so to speak, wider spaces between Middle English than between Modern English words. Although an organic simile would better stress the interdependence of parts, one might say that medieval poems are like the Big Dipper, with its handful of widely spaced points in clear outline; modern poems are more like the densely clustered Milky Way. A medieval poem may qualify its nouns by context just as elaborately as a modern poem, but since the context is larger and less tightly unified, each noun must fit into a looser structure and consequently suffer losses in vivid particularity. Medieval tapers are simply "Bryte," and nothing more is done to strengthen the sense of their brightness.

The Middle English abstract and social nouns can, however, receive certain kinds of qualification from adjectives. The following

* I use "moral" in the broad sense of "evaluative," but still with "moral" connotations.

epigram from the middle of the fourteenth century has a greater proportion of adjectives than usual, but they are of the usual type:

Kyndeli° is now mi coming   *natural*
in to þis [werld] wiht teres and cry;
Litel and pouere is myn hauing,
4   briȝel° and sone i-falle from hi;   *brittle, fragile*
Scharp and strong is my deying,
i ne woth° whider schal i;   *know*
Fowl and stinkande is my roting—
8   on me, ihesu, ȝow haue mercy!

Although this is a first-person complaint about the vanity of existence, all the adjectives occur in third-person statements. The poet even bends the syntax to achieve this effect; instead of the normal "All þat I have is litel and pouer," he writes "Litel and pouere is myn hauing." The adjectives all describe processes in which the poet is involved, but they could easily have modified the subject "I" as predicate adjectives or adverbs. That they are used in third-person constructions is typical of a strong tendency in these poems to avoid speaking directly of one's own affective states.

The adjectives themselves are evenly graded on a scale of intensity from the neutral "Kyndeli" to the very strong "Fowl and stinkande." The intensity is of two sorts, sensuous and evaluative. "Kyndeli" has only the most general sensuous overtones, suggesting as it does the world of nature in contrast to the world of the spirit. Whatever hint of disapproval it contains is a result of the same contrast: the natural world is relatively untrustworthy. "Litel and pouere" are more sensuous, insofar as "pouere" suggests a physical shabbiness, and they are definitely though mildly disapproving. "Briȝel" has a vivid tactile quality, and it suggests the fragility of all worldly things, a sense heavily reinforced by "sone i-falle from hi." "Scharp and strong," by looking ahead to the olfactory reference of the last two adjectives, are equally intense on both the physical and moral scales. The last two adjectives, "Fowl and stinkande," speak for themselves.

These descriptive adjectives gain much of their power from rhythm and position: eight of them occur in symmetrical pairs at the beginnings of lines, in parallel syntactic constructions, and they are arranged on a scale of increasing intensity. This kind of structural context is a medieval equivalent of the dense specification in the Wilbur poem. Otherwise these adjectives, abstract and moral as they are, resemble the others discussed earlier. Most of them express the poet's disapproval, and all are spread over a very wide area—the earthly career of Everyman rather than a few moments in that career—and so are not sharply modified by context.

There are good reasons why the abstract and social nouns, with their attendant adjectives, are not subtle and specific. Because the poems are generally applicable, to classes of people and recurrent situations, they must exclude everything unique or highly particular. They cannot deal with the refinements of personal experience, which are by definition private and not precisely repeatable. Consequently, the nouns in these lyrics remain sufficiently general and unmodified to fit a great many persons, situations, and specific meanings. The precise meaning of "avoid sin," for example, can vary according to circumstances, as it was meant to do.

Metaphor: Tenors

Some of the prominent nouns are modified figuratively, as a rule by some kind of metaphor. In this discussion "metaphor" will be used in the Aristotelian sense, which covers several kinds of meaning-transfer, including metonymy and synecdoche: "Metaphora in the sense of *transference, the process of transferring a word from one object of reference to another* is defined in *Poetics*, 21, 1457b: 'Metaphor consists in applying to a thing a word that belongs to something else; the transference being either from genus to species or from species to genus or from species to species or on grounds of analogy.' "[6] There will be occasions for specifying metonymy or synecdoche, but for the most part such distinctions are not important in the Middle English short poem. It is more important to explain why there are so few kinds of figurative speech than to distinguish sharply among the kinds that do occur.

Under this broad definition of metaphor it is also possible to include allegory and symbolism, since both of these involve meaning-transfer. Allegory is "a narrative [very brief in the Middle English poems] in which the agents, and sometimes the setting as well, represent general concepts, moral qualities, or other abstractions" (Abrams, p. 2). And a symbol, "in the broadest use of the term, is anything which signifies something else; in this sense, all words are symbols. As commonly used in criticism, however, 'symbol' is applied only to a word or phrase signifying an object which itself has significance; that is, the object referred to has a range of meaning [public or private] beyond itself" (Abrams, p. 95). I will use "metaphor," then, for all of these transferences, and distinguish among them only when necessary.

The subjects a poet chooses to treat metaphorically are significant because they form a special class: they are subjects that the standard nonmetaphorical language cannot precisely label. To say that death is a tyrant assumes that the experience of tyranny is more familiar and comprehensible than the experience of death. As Winifred Nowottny has argued, "it would seem to be implied . . . that metaphor would be particularly useful for dealing with phenomena and experiences not so far named by common language."[7] Quite clearly, very large areas of experience are almost beyond the reach of words: subtle emotions, sensory phenomena (especially tastes and smells), or large, necessarily elusive concepts. Middle English verse is notably poor in emotional nuances, and renders only the most obvious sensory experience; but it deals in the largest possible concepts, personal and abstract.

In poems based, for example, on the insight that the world and the flesh cannot be trusted, the most common tenors (the principal subjects of metaphors) are mankind, life, death, and the world, of which death occurs twice as often as any of the other three. This is not surprising, in view of what the poems are trying to say. It is, however, distinctively medieval that the tenors should be such vast, profound, and abstract concepts. The theology of the time, popular and academic, was thoroughly metaphysical and concerned itself with very large problems, such as "mankind, life, death, and the world."

"Life," for instance, covers an almost infinite variety of ideas. At its most abstract, it means just the condition of being alive; medieval schoolmen used terms of comparable abstraction. The difficulty with life as an object of metaphor is plainly a result of its sheer magnitude and complexity, not of its subtlety, as in these lines from Wallace Stevens' "Sunday Morning":

> She dreams a little, and she feels the dark
> Encroachment of that old catastrophe,
> As a calm darkens among water-lights.[8]

The metaphor in the third line, minutely qualified by its rhythm, tells us with great precision what the dreamer has perceived; in fact the subject of this metaphor, the woman's very subtle perception of "that old catastrophe," cannot be named except by the metaphor itself.[9] Life, on the other hand, can certainly be named, but it eludes our grasp because it means too many things, not because it means something too fleeting and subjective. Of course the meaning of "life" is qualified by context, but its high level of generality still keeps it vague. It is different in kind from the tenor of Stevens' metaphor, and different in a typically medieval way.

Many other tenors are in some sense personal nouns, but they are no less large and abstract than words like man or life: for example, God, Christ, the poet's mistress, the Virgin Mary, or the poet as lover, penitent, etc. Christ and Mary are particular, historic persons, but they are quite different in kind from the woman whose consciousness Wallace Stevens portrays in "Sunday Morning." They represent large cultural values, not individual personalities full of interesting problems. Among the many synonyms for Christ are "the Word," "salvation," "the King," "the way, the truth, and the light"; Mary is "the Mother of God," "the Empress of Heaven."[10] These terms are about as vast as life, death, and the world. Despite the Franciscan success in making devotion more personal than it had been,[11] the Middle English poets speak of Christ and the Virgin as wellsprings of infinite value for mankind, not as unique and interesting personalities. This means that as subjects for metaphors, they posed problems similar to the problems attending life, death, and the rest.

Concrete Nouns

A concrete noun "refers to particular, perceivable things and situations" (Abrams, p. 1), which need not be especially vivid or sensuous. The term is distinct from social and personal nouns and, of course, from abstract nouns. The general function of concrete nouns in the medieval poems is illustrative. These nouns are used to support practical intentions; they are not objects of interest in their own right, as they often are in modern poetry. (I shall speak of the nouns and their referents interchangeably, only distinguishing the two if confusion would otherwise result.) The following lines by Ezra Pound are very unmedieval in their use of concrete nouns:

Birds with flowery wing, hovering butterflies
    crowd over the thousand gates,
Trees that glitter like jade,
    terraces tinged with silver,
The seed of a myriad hues,
A net-work of arbors and passages and covered ways,
Double towers, winged roofs,
    border the net-work of ways:
A place of felicitous meeting.[12]

Pound is interested, here and elsewhere, in concrete particulars for their own sake; he is not using them to illustrate the abstract idea of "felicitous meeting," as a medieval poet would have done. For Pound, the concrete words are primary, and the abstract phrase "a place of felicitous meeting" serves to modify them. For the medieval poet, abstractions of various kinds are the subject matter, which concrete nouns help to explain:

Quan I cum fro þe plow at non,
In a reuen° dych myn mete is don;   *cracked, riven*
I dar not askyn our dame a spon—
    I dar not [seyn° quan che seyȝt 'pes!']   *speak*

The plow suggests the husband's hard and honest labor; the meat in the cracked dish reveals him as cruelly abused and long-suffering; and the spoon again points to the wife's petty contempt for her guiltless husband. All the concrete nouns are subordinate to ideas and attitudes, and they are stated flatly, with very little modification. The poet is not interested in the sensuous value or even the quiddity of plows, cracked dishes, and so forth (see p. 78 for the full text).

Most concrete nouns in the poems are drawn from three publicly accessible areas of daily reality: they refer to common artifacts, nature, and human affairs. Some of the nouns are metaphoric vehicles, but they do not differ in kind from the rest; metaphoric or not, most concrete nouns are illustrative, and all are more or less ordinary. Besides the dish and spoon mentioned above, the poems contain the following artifacts and common foods: cup, clothes, window, bower, bread, staff, bed, flesh (meat), cheese, peas, penny, spade, scythe, flail, wine, chain, seat, bells, chalice, crown, tapers, various drapes and hangings, stocks, puddings, sauce, fish, ale, (food-) bin, gold, incense,

nails, shoe, drink, bench, floor, pit, and shield. Among the larger artifacts are several kinds of buildings: tower, hall, chapel, and castle.

All of these words are relatively commonplace and large; they
do not refer to rare or specialized items such as a particular kind of
Provençal sausage or parts of a bishop's vestment. Even the more exotic nouns—chalice, crown, incense, gold—would not have been unfamiliar to people with access to a good-sized church or a cathedral.[18]
And, as usual, these nouns are not heavily modified.

Another important source of concrete nouns is the realm of nature, which was no less available to medieval men than the contents of
their houses and churches. Here are some "natural" nouns from these
lyrics, listed in many cases with their direct modifiers: daylight, green
leaf, "wode-gore" (forest plot, or perhaps foliage),[14] moor, violet,
"chilled waters of the well-spring," rush (reed), fire, lands, birds in
bough, corn, meadow, wheat, swine, seed, ewe, lamb, May morning,
red rose, bullock, sun, buck, falcon, stone, lily flower, cuckoo, "or-
chard brown," moon, mire, fair weather, filth, worm's meat, worms,
primrose, turf, pit, hounds, fields, blast (of wind), night, "treo"
(wood), wood (forest), ice, and earth.

Concrete nouns for both artificial and natural objects are broad in
meaning, and ordinary. There are, of course, differences among them,
based on the subjects and intentions of the poems in which they occur:
contemptus poems include inventories of decaying parts of the body
and many referents concerned with burial, such as earth, coffin, and
shroud; feast songs naturally refer to foods and drinks; love poems
often list kinds of jewelry or clothing and parts of the lady's body;
passion poems speak of the cross, the nails, and Christ's suffering
body; religious or secular love poems use nature imagery; and so forth.
But even where differences exist in specific vocabulary, they are differences among subdivisions of the same general category: broad,
everyday, largely unmodified words about physical reality. To demonstrate the local and special quality of this very commonplace diction,
I shall quote from a stylistic alternative, perhaps the polar opposite of
the Middle English short poem:

> Nota: man is the intelligence of his soil,
> The sovereign ghost. As such, the Socrates
> Of snails, musician of pears, principium
> 4   And lex. Sed quaeritur: is this same wig

Of things, this nincompated pedagogue,
Preceptor to the sea? Crispin at sea
Created, in his day, a touch of doubt.
8 An eye most apt in gelatines and jupes,
Berries of villages, a barber's eye,
An eye of land, of simple salad-beds,
Of honest quilts, the eye of Crispin, hung
12 On porpoises, instead of apricots,
And on silentious porpoises, whose snouts
Dibbled in waves that were mustachios,
Inscrutable hair in an inscrutable world.

These are the opening lines from "The Comedian as the Letter C" by Wallace Stevens,[15] a poem about the relationships among everyday reality, exotic reality, and the poet's imagination. Although this passage deals with ordinary experience, especially in lines 8 through 12, it could hardly be more unlike Middle English verse in its diction. The concrete words and phrases are neither commonplace nor unmodified, nor are they earthbound ("The sovereign ghost," "The Socrates/ Of snails," etc.). It would even take some elaborate rationalizing to fit both the Stevens and an apposite medieval poem under one rubric such as "verses about everyday reality," though this could ultimately be done, and legitimately. In any case, the diction of the medieval English poems, from Stevens' point of view, would be unnatural indeed.

Metaphor: Vehicles

I have so far discussed concrete nouns without distinguishing those that occur in metaphors from those that do not. There is actually little difference. Most concrete nouns are of the types I have listed; they refer to artifacts or natural objects, whether or not they are used metaphorically. This also holds true for the third main class of concrete words, those referring to human affairs or activities; but since their metaphoric use is distinctively important, I shall give it special attention.

It is also true that words about activities are often verbs or verbal expressions rather than concrete nouns, although the distinction is not absolute. I have argued elsewhere that most verbs in the short poems are generalized, hence colorless; but there are certain mild exceptions. Verbs that are intransitive by nature or by usage are the least vivid of all: die, live, kiss, drink, spend, sing, be glad, pray, make merry, eat, weeping, sigh, mourn, fall, laugh. Transitive verbs naturally involve substantives—fill the cup, she breaks my head, I warm my hands, I flail the grain—and are vivid to that extent. But nearly all the verbs of action, unlike the pure connectives, are on the same level of generality as the nouns I have discussed, and for the same reasons.

Metaphors and concrete nouns in the short poems are similar in that both modify abstract and social nouns; but when the concrete nouns occur in metaphors, they are normally vehicles, not tenors. The most striking feature of these metaphoric vehicles is that many are almost self-sufficient as metaphors. If we see that the unknown subject is metaphorically a fresh fountain (which is life-giving) or a polished gem (which is precious and beautiful), we already know a great deal about it. We might even guess who is being described.* When a medieval poet speaks of anything "fading like a green leaf," we can guess even more confidently that he is talking about man or the world of nature. To some extent we understand these references because they have become clichés since the Middle Ages or were proverbial even then; nevertheless, vehicles like daylight, a polished gem, and fading like green leaves do identify their tenors with considerable precision. To do this, they must be either qualified (fading like a green leaf) or have a quite specific, limited meaning or function (worm's meat).

All of this applies with special force to words that denote common human activities (words referring to natural processes are quite rare).† The metaphoric second terms drawn from human affairs fall into two main categories: social-institutional and physical activities. The following second terms from the lyrics are based on social phenomena: putting an offering in the collection box, assizes, journey, battle, cherry-fair, check-mate, stealing a flower, domain (political power), love-making, marriage, buying and selling, thrall versus free, and (royal) court. Physical activities or nonactivities include standing and falling, rest, wandering, being cast down, falling from a bench, binding (someone), catching one's foot in a wheel, climbing high, and striking at a shield.

* If the vehicle is a type or title of Mary or Christ, our guess will be almost infallible (see note 10).

† Some examples are the growing of grass, leaping bucks (13th:6), and the turning and falling of leaves (14th:9)—all quite "commonplace and general," and reasonably self-explanatory as vehicles.

These vehicles too are almost all commonplace and general, and many are intelligible in themselves. But their independence of meaning has a slightly different basis from that of the artifacts and natural things discussed above. Only a few seem essentially metaphorical (e.g., a journey); most of the rest are so close to describing the actual state of affairs, or so dead as metaphors, that they have the effect of literal statements.

To speak of being cast down, for example, if the context ensures a figurative interpretation, is practically the same as saying that "misfortune (death, for instance), like a mighty wrestler, casts us down." The first term of the metaphor is implicit in the second. This is also true of human life as metaphorically "wandering," of disaster as "falling from a bench," and so on. All of these, and many others, are actually or nearly proverbial, and they have faded so badly that one can hardly tell whether they are figurative or literal.

It is difficult to say exactly why the metaphoric vehicles based on human affairs should seem more self-explanatory than those referring to artifacts or nature. I would guess, however, that this derives from the realities involved: human actions are usually more intelligible than artifacts or the things of nature because they represent human intentions and experience. To another human being their meanings are often self-evident, whereas the meaning of a natural event or object is not intuitively obvious. Nor can a rose or even a broken dish be related as precisely to human experience as a journey or the last move in a chess game, because the latter two *are* human experiences; the desired relationship may be left implicit, and need not require laborious exposition.

Except for this peculiarity of the vehicles drawn from human affairs, the three sources of material for metaphors are not distinctive (aside from distinctions based on the uniqueness of nature, artifacts, or human activities). All the metaphoric vehicles, like the diction of these poems, are relatively commonplace and general; and they are more or less intelligible without the first term, or tenor, of the metaphor.

Metaphor: Symbolism and Metonymy

The second terms of medieval metaphors can be self-sufficient in another way: they can be symbols, or symbolic metonymies, whose figurative sense is embedded in medieval culture and therefore obvious (to anyone familiar with that culture) in isolation from the first terms. This form of quasi-trope is especially medieval, insofar as it seems more factual and blunt than figurative. Its form is indeed perfectly direct and unmetaphorical, but it is actually a kind of metonymy. For example:

> Uuere beþ þey biforen vs weren,[1]
> Houndes ladden and hauekes beren[2]
> And hadden feld and wode?
> 4 Þe riche leuedies in hoere bour,
> Þat wereden gold in hoere tressour°   *hair bands*
> Wiþ hoere briȝtte rode;°   *complexions*
>
> Eten and drounken and maden hem glad;
> 8 Hoere lif was al wiþ gamen° I-lad,   *pleasure*
> Men keneleden hem biforen,   *kneeled before them*
> Þey beren hem wel swiþe heye—[3]
> And in a twincling of on eye
> 12 Hoere soules weren forloren.
>
> Were is þat lawing° and þat song,   *laughter*
> Þat trayling° and þat proude ȝong,°   *trailing long garments; gait*
> Þo hauekes and þo houndes?
> 16 Al þat ioye is went away,
> Þat wele is comen te weylaway,°   *(an exclamation of despair)*
> To manie harde stoundes.°   *pangs*
>
> Hoere paradis hy nomen here,   *They took their paradise here*
> 20 And nou þey lien in helle I-fere,°   *together*
> Þe fuir hit brennes heuere
> Long is ay and long is ho,
> Long is wy and long is wo—
> 24 Þennes ne comeþ þey neuere.

(13th:48)

The approach is factual and true to life; no doubt wealthy Englishmen of the thirteenth century did have hawks and hounds, and they must have sung and laughed on occasion. It is important that these details be historically accurate, but accuracy is only a prerequisite; they are important mainly because they suggest a whole way of life which

---

[1] *Where are those who were before us*
[2] *Who led hounds and carried hawks*
[3] *They bore themselves very high (haughtily)*

the poet wants to condemn. Because the physical details are used as *pars pro toto*, they are not sharply described. Since they function only as pointers or reminders, vivid description would be irrelevant.

The same kind of symbolism can be found in some of the devotional poems,[16] because the objects and events in sacred history had acquired traditional meanings. In these lines, for instance, Christ addresses Everyman from the cross:

> þi garland is of grene,
> of floures many on;°   *many a one*
> Myn of sharpe þornes,
> My hewe it makeþ won.°   *wan*
>   (14th:126)

The garland of thorn in this poem represents all the suffering of God for mankind, as the hawks and hounds and green garland represent the self-indulgence of mankind. Similarly, the boar's head is more than just a piece of meat:

> The boris hed In hondes I brynge,
> With garlondes gay & byrdes syngynge!
> I pray you all helpe me to synge,
>   Qui estis in convivio.   *who are at this feast*

The boar's head clearly stands for and evokes the spirit of festivity; the poet has no need of explanation or sharp description.

All of these metonymies conceal figurative intentions in the guise of factual reports. They inform us, in effect, that keeping hawks and hounds implies mortal sin, that wearing a crown of thorns implies infinite suffering, and that a boar's head, as one item in a recipe for merry-making, signifies the whole proceedings. In each case, the concrete noun is a symbol pointing to a much wider significance.

Metaphor: Allegories and Riddles

The meaning of a symbolic metonymy must, then, be explicit and precise, and it must be part of the general culture, not unique to the particular text. It is in keeping with the public nature of the short poems that their tropes should be clear and accessible, but they need not accomplish this by referring beyond the poem to wide areas of commonly accepted meaning. On the contrary, two important kinds

of metaphor, the miniature allegory and the riddle, define their meaning, explicitly and at length, within the bounds of the poem itself. Both
are essentially metaphorical because they describe one reality (the
tenor) in terms appropriate to another (the vehicle); and in both, the
several parts of the tenor and vehicle are symmetrically related to each
other, in a way that suggests the complex symmetry of allegorical
trees.[17]

It is often hard to distinguish, in particular cases, between miniature allegories (henceforth simply called allegories) and riddles. In
general, however, the meaning of an allegory is clear, even explicit,
whereas the essence of a riddle is the darkness of its meaning, a darkness it achieves by omitting any reference to the real tenor. In "Al nist
by þe rose," for instance, the vehicle is given but the tenor is to be
guessed:

Al nist° by þe rose, rose—	*night*
al nist bi the rose i lay;	
darf ich noust þe rose stele,	*I dared not steal the rose*
ant ȝet ich bar þe flour away.	

We know only that the speaker lay all night by a rose which he dared
not steal but which he did "deflower." What is the meaning of this?
We must use our imaginations.

Allegories and riddles are public devices because, like symbolic
times extend throughout the poem. But here I shall discuss only those
that extend no further than a few lines, because their kinship with
other kinds of metaphor lessens as their length increases. (For a discussion of allegories and riddles as overall principles of order, see
Chapter 6.) The following are typical:

A.   ser Iohn to me Is proferyng
           ffor hys plesure ryght well to pay,
          & In my box he puttes hys offryng—
           (I haue no powre to say hym nay.)
                         (14/15th:26)

B. Ihesu cryst, myn leman° swete,		*beloved*
ȝat[1] for me deye-des° on rode tre,		*died*
Wiht al myn herte i ȝe bi-seke		
4 for ȝi wndes° to and thre,		*wounds*

---

[1] *that (þ is represented throughout by ȝ);*

> ʒat al so faste in myn herte
> ʒi loue roted mute be,[2]
> as was ʒe spere in-to ʒi side,
> 8 whan ʒow suffredis ded° for me.   *death*

> C.   To-day I sat full ryall in a cheyere,
> Tyll sotell deth knokyd at my gate,
> And on-avysed° he seyd to me, chek-mate!   *without warning*
>   (15th:149)

In each of these, the tenor is an action or process rather than the usual substantive. (In this respect, the three passages are characteristically medieval: when a medieval poet writes figuratively about actions or processes, he tends to use an allegory instead of a one-term vehicle.[18]) And in each, the two poles of the comparison, both consisting of several parts, are parallel point for point. The first is a riddle, whose meaning is unmistakable in context. When we realize that a young lady is speaking of fornication, we have no trouble identifying the box and the offering. The second passage is an allegory in which the speaker's (figurative) heart and Christ's love are related to Christ's (actual) heart and the soldier's spear. The comparison is especially apt, since the pangs of love, traditionally likened to the thrust of a blade, here become the actual blade that entered Christ's heart because of his love for us. The spear has a threefold, intertwined meaning: it represents the historical spear, Christ's love for us, and, we pray, our love for him. The third excerpt contains a miniature allegory and a dead metaphor. The approach of death is the knock at the gate; the victim caught *in media vita* is the man sitting "full royally" in his house; and the moment of death is the "chek-mate!" (We are not being asked to imagine that Death and Everyman had been playing chess: "chek-mate!" simply means "the game's over—you lose.")

Allegories and riddles are public devices because, like symbolic metonymy, their meanings are deliberately obvious; even the riddles, whose meanings must be partly hidden, are more like double entendres than like the often truly obscure Anglo-Saxon riddles. Whether it is arbitrary or really describes its tenor,[19] the allegory, like a sermon or a scholastic treatise, makes its meaning explicit piece by piece. This method is well suited to a poetry of exposition which, based on com-

---

[2] *thy love might be rooted*

mon values, is aimed at broad groups of people. It is natural, therefore, that allegories should occur among the often discursive poems of
persuasion and definition, but not among the celebratory poems.

Puns, Paradox, and Denotation

The same reliance on explicit statement rather than suggestion
also shows itself in the frequent use of puns and paradox throughout
the short poems. Of course puns and paradoxes may be difficult, even
subtle, but not in the modern way:

> The monsoon cut across the delta
> At gulf gates . . . There, beyond the dykes
>
> I heard wind flaking sapphire, like this summer,
> And willows could not hold more steady sound.[20]

These lines by Hart Crane, apparently referring to the Mississippi
estuary below New Orleans, are subtle and difficult because they depend heavily on connotations, which are much more subjective and
less exact than denotations. "Sapphire" suggests the hard, brilliant,
and precious blue of the sea and its reflection in the sky; "flaking" suggests a delicate, measured attrition between the wind and sapphire sea
(bits of foam and spray), and also between the wind and the reeds,
pointing back to the first stanza ("The willows carried a slow sound,/
A sarabande the wind mowed on the mead / . . . That seething, steady
leveling of the marshes") and forward to the last line. And attrition, by
suggesting the pervasive heat of summer and sky, binds "summer" and
"sapphire" by further associations.

My reading of these highly evocative lines is disputable, precisely
because the lines are evocative and inexplicit. In Middle English poems,
however, the corresponding difficulties of meaning, in puns and paradoxes, are quite straightforward, since they are based on denotations.
Paronomasia, one of the many rhetorical devices set forth by the writing manuals and practiced by the Middle English poets, is "a play on
words that are identical or similar in sound but have sharply diverse
meanings; or it is the use of a single word or phrase with two incon-
gruous meanings, both relevant" (Abrams, p. 37). It is important to
add that "meanings" in both cases refers only to denotative meanings.

Recent studies have dealt with the significance of puns in such lyrics as "Nou goth sonne vnder wod,"* "Foweles in the frith," and "Wel, qwa sal thir hornes blau."[21] In each of these poems, and in many others, the puns point to ambiguities inherent in the subject matter. For instance, the whole epigram "Leerne, þou vnkynde man, to be kynde" is based on the double meaning of kynde as "nature" and "kindness":

> Leerne, þou vnkynde man, to be kynde°   *natural, kind*
> of a beest þat haþ no skille° of kynde.   *reason*
> Hou þou doist schame to þi kynde,
> but þou to ihū crist be kynde!

The pun is not merely frivolous: the only natural way to treat Christ is to treat him kindly. Also, the opening line of the famous "I syng of a myden þat is makeles" (p. 83) contains a pun on makeles as "peerless" and "mateless," two related attributes of Mary that are crucially important for the poem and for the human race.[22] Most other puns, including equivoques, are likewise built on the primary meanings of very important words.

Paradox, like punning, is radically denotative; its effectiveness depends wholly on the situation it refers to, not on verbal nuances. Paradoxes are essentially puns based on a sharp opposition between the literal and nonliteral meanings of a word: "Sen þat þi [literally, 'human'] sone þi [figuratively, 'divine'] fader Is." In these words addressed to Mary the poet catches up one of the central paradoxes inherent in his faith:

> Haill! quene of hevin & steren° of blis;   *star*
> Sen° þat þi sone þi fader Is,   *since*
> How suld he ony thing þe warn,°   *deny*
> 4 And thou his mothir and he þi barne?°   *child*
>
> Haill! fresche fontane þat springis new,
> The rute and crope of all vertu,
> Thou polist° gem without offence,   *polished*
> 8 Thou bair þe Lambe of Innocence.

---

* In this lyric, as in others of the Middle English tradition, the puns are intended to support primary meanings, not to display the poet's ingenuity:

Nou goth sonne vnder wod,°—   *wood (a forest, the cross)*
me reweth, marie, þi faire Rode.°   *complexion*
Nou goþ sonne vnder tre,°—   *trees, cross*
me reweþ, marie, þi sone and þe.

Paradox is also built into the very nature of other important poetic subgenres. The mortality poets, for example, never tired of what may be called the mortal paradox, and they repeated it, with variations, again and again: in spite of all appearances, "this too too solid flesh will melt, / Thaw, and resolve itself into a dew"—except that a medieval poet would specify that in fact flesh resolves itself into carrion. Equally alien to common sense is the Christian paradox based on the Incarnation, which so many songwriters celebrated: that God is man, that Omnipotence has taken the shape of a baby, with all that this implies. And the courtly lovers declare, almost in the vein of moralists, that life without a compliant mistress is really not life, but a form of death:

This ys no lyf, alas, þat y do lede;
it is but deth as yn lyves lyckenesse
(14/15th:165)

My deþ y loue, my lyf ich hate, for a leudy shene°   *beautiful*
(13th:85)

In the first passage, "lyf" really means "enjoyable, good life," and "lyves" refers to ordinary, minimal life, which in the absence of love resembles death, where "deth" is the opposite of "lyf"; "deth" means, in general, "unpleasant life," not literal death, and so does not contrast with "lyves." Both passages reflect the ambivalence of courtly love: it is both sweet and sour.

The vanity poems, as I have said, also contain many actual if not formal paradoxes. There is no need to catalog examples; it will suffice to point out that any *ubi sunt* poem necessarily implies the mortal paradox. The poet knows he can shock his audience merely by stating that Helen, Alexander, and the rest were once as alive as you, the audience, but now they are dust. Furthermore, everyone who today is loved and pampered, by himself and his family, will become tomorrow a loathsome object that no one would want to embrace. Our strong sense of permanence, even immortality, is a cruel lie. The truth is almost inconceivable.

Most paradoxes in the celebratory poems derive from the nature of Christ. Each of these excerpts views the Incarnation from a slightly different angle:

A. That child ys God, that child is man
   And in that child oure lif bygan.
      (C:12)

B. For in this rose [Mary] conteynyd was
   Heuen and erthe in lytyl space
      (C:173)

C. kyng of alle kynges to here sone che ches° *chose*
      (15th:81)

D. A God and yet a man?
    A mayde and yet a mother?
   Witt wonders what witt Can
 4 Conceave this or the other.

   A god, and Can he die?
    A dead man, can he live?
   What witt can well replie?
 8 What reason reason give?

   God, truth itselfe, doth teach it;
    Mans witt senckis too farr vnder
   By reasons power to reach it.
 12 Beleeve and leave to wonder!

E. When he was borne that made all thyng
      (C:23B)

Each paradox is implicit in the meaning of the Incarnation, which, as the point of juncture between everyday and transcendent reality, is itself a kind of existential pun as well as paradox. The fifth excerpt is typically complex: since God made all things, how could He have been born? Did He create himself, too, or exist from eternity? In any case, what is meant by the "birth" of God in time? This line suggests all the complexity of trinitarian thought, as well as the doctrines of creation and the eternity of God.

 The Virgin Mary and the eucharistic bread were also inherently paradoxical, but they attracted far less poetic attention than the central mystery of Christ. (Of course Mary's uniqueness has value only with respect to Christ, and the communion bread *is* Christ, so both actually represent the same problem.) Here, paradox takes the riddle form:

Hyt semes quite,° and is red:	*white*
Hyt is quike° and semes dede:	*quick, alive*
Hyt is fleshe and semes bred:	
4 Hyt is one and semes too:	
Hyt is God° body and no mo.	*God's*

The equivocation is based on the gulf between sensuous and metaphysical truth, between appearance and reality; the bread is "red" and "quike" figuratively, except that in this case what seems figurative (redness and liveness) is really true on a higher level than sense-perception. The fifth line, although it approaches epigrammatic pointedness, is actually much more medieval than Augustan. It logically concludes the argument, and makes the content of the paradoxes explicit.

The paradox of Mary deserves further mention. She is both mother and virgin; consequently, her ritual purification, on the last day of the Christmas season,[23] is a contradiction in terms. As the poet says, she came "Vnto the temple with hyr chyld / To shew hyr clen that neuer was fyled" (c:8). Like the other paradoxes, this one is doctrinal in content and balanced in form; but it does not attempt the kind of wit associated with seventeenth-century metaphysical poets, or with eighteenth-century writers of heroic couplets. Paradox, in general, is very well suited to expressing the medieval world view; the truth is transcendent, whether it is the transcendent fact of death, or the divine nature of a human baby, or the virginity of God's mother.

Intensifiers

I shall use *intensifier* not in its standard grammatical sense, but in the sense of "a word or group of words that underscores the intention of a poem." Since these poems have the practical aim of affecting people's lives, their intensifiers are basically imperative; they supply authority and comprehensiveness. The first of these functions is carried out mostly by proverbial language, including commonplaces and formulas that approach the condition of proverbs. The second function, lending comprehensiveness, is accomplished by words of magnitude, positive or negative.

A standard definition of *proverb* points to its source of authority and suggests its use: a proverb is "a concise sentence, which is held to express some truth ascertained by experience or observation and familiar to all."[24] Proverbs are familiar to all because they originate in common experience, which they serve to define, often by prescribing general modes of behavior. Proverbs thus carry the massive weight of folk wisdom, an authority which, in times of overwhelming illiteracy, must have seemed nearly absolute.[25] A poem gained immense strength from such statements as these:

A. ʒef þou in my boure art take, shame þe may bityde.
    þe is bettere on fote gon,[1] þen wycked hors to ryde
    (13th:25)

B. Spende, and god schal sende;
    spare, and ermor care;
    non peni, non ware;
    non catel,° non care.   *property*
       go, peni, go.

C. She seith þat she hath seyn it write
    That "seldyn seyn is sone for-geit."
    (14/15th:171)

D. Man mei longe him liues wene,[2]
    ac ofte him liyet þe wreinch;[3]
    fair weder ofte him went° to rene,   *turns*
       an ferliche maket is blench.[4]
    (13th:10A)

Each of these generalizations modifies a different intention. In the first, a girl is advising her clerical lover to keep his distance, rather than risk being caught with her and suffering shame; the second is a piece of practical advice; the third, put in the mouth of the poet's far-away mistress, is quoted only to be denied (he, will, on the contrary, never forget her); and the proverbs in the fourth passage refer to the well known mutability of human affairs. Yet for all their obvious differences, these intentions, and the proverbs that support them, share "general applicability." Some poems are, indeed, no more nor less than expanded proverbs.

Commonplaces and formulas also give authority to poems, but

---

[1] *it is better for thee to go on foot*
[2] *Man may expect to have a long life*
[3] *but often the "twist" is lying in wait for him*
[4] *and suddenly plays its trick*

their effect is somewhat different from that of proverbs, perhaps because their source is to be found in classical rhetoric rather than popular English wisdom. Of the five main divisions of rhetoric, invention (*inventio*) is the most important. And of the five divisions of invention, the evidence (*argumentio*) is most important for our purposes, because it involves the use of commonplaces or *topoi*. E. R. Curtius has succinctly defined the *topos* (I shall use the English *commonplace*) and its function within a narrative (*narratio*):

> Essentially, every oration (including panegyrics) must make some proposition or thing plausible. It must adduce in its favor arguments which address themselves to the hearer's mind or heart. Now, there is a whole series of such arguments, which can be used on the most diverse occasions. They are intellectual themes, suitable for development and modification at the orator's pleasure. . . . To elucidate its meaning—a topos of the most general sort is "emphasis on inability to do justice to the subject"; a topos of panegyric: "praise of forebears and their deeds". . . . Originally, then, topoi are helps toward composing orations. They are, as Quintilian . . . says, "storehouses of trains of thought" ("argumentorum sedes"), and thus can serve a practical purpose. . . . They become clichés, which can be used in any form of literature, they spread to all spheres of life with which literature deals and to which it gives form.[26]

Commonplaces and formulas are the building blocks of classical orations and of medieval poems as well. By formula I mean a phrase that recurs more or less verbatim, such as "wit and wisdom" or "make ye merry both all and some"; it need not be a complete thought, although it may be. There is no absolute distinction between commonplaces and stock metaphors. Both are recurrent, and commonplaces may be figurative, but a commonplace must amplify a larger theme, such as "remember death" or "praise Christ." The formula may of course be distinguished from both by its persistent verbal identity. The following is a fair sample of commonplaces and formulas:

1. let everyone drink to his companion (14/15th:3)
2. lament of the seduced maiden (14/15th:27)
3. marriage is to be avoided (wives are shrewish, greedy, etc.) (14/15th:43)
4. the lover pleads absolute loyalty to his mistress (14/15th:171)

5. superlative praise of Mary's virtue and beauty (15th:45)
6. Welcome, Christmas! (C:5)
7. Lady Fortune turns her wheel (14th:42)
8. since Christ suffered and died for us, we should abandon sin for Christ (14th:126)
9. the certainty of death versus the uncertainty when and whither (13th:12B)
10. *ubi sunt* (13th:48)

All of these are intellectual themes if we take "intellectual" in a broad enough sense; and all are "suitable for development and modification at the [poet's] pleasure." Aside from examples 6 and 10, all—even the first—may provide the thematic structure for whole poems; but for the most part, they are used as building blocks, like examples 6 and 10. Because the medieval lyrics are general and impersonal, these blocks need not be cut into unique shapes for unique purposes; the poet can shift them about at will, like interchangeable parts. In this they resemble the proverbs, which can apply to a great many specific situations. But unlike proverbs, the commonplaces and formulas often give reasons for their authority rather than assuming it: examples 2, 3, 4, 7, 8, and 9 carry at least implicit arguments, and examples 5 and 10 are normally supported by description, whereas a typical proverb is gnomic and simply true.

As usual, the medieval approach appears more distinctive when contrasted with modern ways of thinking and writing. Even when a modern poet like Gerard Manley Hopkins uses a traditional medieval trope in writing about death, the effect is very unmedieval:

> Márgarét, are you grléving
> Over Goldengrove unleaving?
> Leáves, like the things of man, you
> With your fresh thoughts care for, can you?
> . . . .
> Nor mouth had, no nor mind, expressed
> What heart heard of, ghost guessed:
> It ís the blight man was born for,
> It is Margaret you mourn for.[27]

This beginning and end of a poem by Hopkins may be compared to the following fourteenth-century winter song:

Wynter wakeneþ al my care,
nou þis leues waxeþ bare;
ofte y sike° & mourne sare[1]   *sigh*
4   when hit comeþ in my þoht
     of þis worldes ioie hou hit geþ al to noht.

Nou hit is & nou hit nys,
also hit ner nere ywys.[2]
8   þat° moni mon seiþ soþ hit ys: *that which*
     "al goþ bote godes wille,
     alle we shule deye þah vs like ylle."[3]

al þat grein me graueþ grene[4]
12   nou hit faleweþ al by-dene—°   *straightway*
     ihesu, help þat hit be sene
     ant shild vs from helle,
     for y not whider y shal ne hou longe her duelle.

The modern poem has the intimate tone of a man speaking to
a young girl; the problem is general, but it is presented apropos of a
particular situation—Margaret's grief over Goldengrove losing its
leaves—and its resolution in the last couplet is suddenly personal and
direct. The medieval poem makes the same connection between falling
leaves and human mortality, but it remains an expository statement,
bare of all feelings except the speaker's "care"; and it puts the crucial
issue in the form of commonplaces (ll. 5, 9–10) and formulas (ll. 6–7,
15), whereas Hopkins, after carefully preparing the way, resolves the
question climactically with a revelation, a diagnosis of what is really
bothering Margaret. Hopkins makes a full statement, rational and
emotional, of the problem of death; the medieval poet supports his
rational statement with only the most general emotions, and prays to
Jesus for help.

A final peculiarity of medieval diction is the prominence of words
denoting comprehensiveness, superlative degrees, extent in space and
time, vastness, finality, and the like. These intensifiers not only have

[1] *sore, very much*
[2] *as if it had never been, certainly*
[3] *we shall all die, though it please us ill*
[4] *all that grain that one buries green (unripe)*

specific syntactic and thematic functions, but they also lend a distinctive flavor to the poems, a flavor quite appropriate to the "big" words they modify, like God, death, and love. Typical words and phrases of this sort are: he has no peer, in every land, all, as merry as we may, every man, whosoever, no more, never, everyone, none, evermore, [no one lives who loves her better than I], both night and day, friend nor foe, ever, in each degree, without variance, eternally, *tota pulchra*, endless, a long way, nevermore, more than one may think, no man, both more and less, naught, both all and some, both old and young, all manner, ne may no man, whole, every foe, without end, never . . . undone, last doom, and all the world.

Many of these words are synonymous and recur frequently (all, everyone, never, etc.); and many occur in pairs, in order to stress their inclusiveness and the absolute validity of the statements they modify. But the words must be seen in context:

A.   Eueriche freman hach[1] to ben hende,[2]
         for to be Large[3] of þat him crist sende;
         þan it es al ydon that cume to þen ende,
         na haues naman of þis werld bot gnedeliche[4] his Lenge.[5]

B.   Worldys blys, haue good day!
         No lengur habbe ych þe ne may,[6]
         þe more for the lesse y haue for-lore;[7]
  4   y-cursyd be þe tyme þat ych was bore!
         y haue lore for-euer heuun blys,
         and go now þeras[8] euer sorow & car ys.

The first of these poems is a very early (perhaps twelfth century) and brief sermon in the third person. As such, it carefully defines its scope: "*Eueriche* freman." The claim is absolute and universal, like most of the moral imperatives on which medieval poems are based. This sense of perfect certainty is intensified in the second half of the

---

[1] *ought*
[2] *gracious*
[3] *generous*
[4] *scarcely*
[5] *length*
[6] *I may no longer have thee*
[7] *lost*
[8] *there where*

argument, where "al ydon" and "þen ende" are equally uncompromising and final, and "ne haues naman," a grammatically negative form of "Eueriche freman," adds a double feeling of negativity to the universal statement. All these phrases refer to unquestionable facts; it is not mere rhetoric to say that everyone will die, and that all mortal activity ceases at death. The poet's words of finality and all-inclusiveness derive great power from their truth to experience.

"Worldys blys," from the fifteenth century, places more stress on the vast, awesome gulf between time and eternity. We feel the sad fragility of each passing moment in the words "No lengur"; even as we pronounce them after the poet, they have disappeared, and with them the moments they contained. The counterpoise to "No lengur" is "for-euer" in line 5, just as "heuun blys" balances "Worldys blys." "For-euer" is especialy poignant in this context, because it precedes "heuun blys," a phrase that it traditionally modifies; yet here it actually modifies the despairing "y haue lore." "No lengur" is also echoed by "now" in line 6, and "euer" repeats "for-euer," though it is used differently. In the last line, "euer" modifies the subsequent rather than the preceding phrase; the effect is to resolve the grammatical situation in line 5, where "for-euer" seems to modify the wrong phrase (it is heaven's bliss that traditionally lasts forever, not one's loss of it). In line 6 "euer" modifies the thematically appropriate phrase ("þeras . . . sorow & care ys"), but the meaning is the same in both lines, and it is more positively, hence more conclusively, stated in the last line.

But the moralists and the prophets of doom are not alone in supporting their intentions with words of magnitude, comprehensiveness, and the like. The courtly lyric clearly lends itself to superlatives: "he leuyth not þat louyd her / so well as y" (14/15th:171). And so, for similar reasons, does the Marian lyric: "In all this worlde ys none so tru / As she that bare our Lorde Jhesu" (Pr:26), or "the myldeste may that euer was mente" (15th:45). The feast songs and Christmas carols also make absolute claims and demands: "Go day, Syre Cristemas, our kyng, / For eueryman, both olde and yynge, / Ys glad and blithe of your comynge" (C:5); "In euery londe ... / Is merthe & gomyn ... / ... a messyngere / ... / Byddes vs all be mere here / ... / let euery mon drynke to hys fere!" (14/15:3). To make his verse as compelling as possible, the medieval English poet used words of magnitude and comprehensiveness—sometimes with sheer force, and sometimes with great subtlety.

Some Conclusions: The Thinness of Figurative Language and Connotations

In my discussion of diction and metaphor, and indeed throughout this study, I have insisted that the intentions of the short poems have determined their style. Thus, from the poets' desire to relate classes of people to particular states of mind, soul, and body, it follows that the poems are markedly substantive; abstract and social nouns, qualified by intensifiers, are the two main poles of meaning. A further corollary, which I have emphasized less, is that denotation is more prominent and more highly developed than connotation. Of course every word has connotations, except bare function-words like *the, an, or,* and the rest; but medieval connotations are relatively general, because the words are not very strongly or affectively modified; the poets do not give us any finely nuanced feelings of their own, and their subjects are not drenched in suggestive particularity. Medieval poems depend heavily for effectiveness on such external criteria as their truth to experience or doctrine. Even the simplest poem about death, for example, has a blunt, archaic force, lacking in all refinement. To read such an epigram is like coming upon a gray stone with a few angular words cut deeply into it: ALL OF YOU WILL DIE.

Denotation suits the intentions of these poems because it is the most publicly available aspect of meaning; connotation, insofar as it derives from the poet's own feelings and attitudes, is private. Because the words explain themselves directly, there is also less need for figurative language than in more evocative poetry. The interesting fact to explain, then, is not the predominance of metaphor among the tropes, but that tropes of any kind are relatively rare, especially in celebratory poems. I have tried to account for those tropes that do occur by relating them to the intentions of the poets and to other cultural forms of the Middle Ages. Thus, paradox was a natural means of representing the Incarnation and the true nature of our apparently solid mortal existence; allegory was also common in theological writings, stained glass windows, sculpture, and elsewhere; and metaphor was a convenient way of relating large, abstract concepts (life, death, love, the Virgin Mary, heaven) to daily experience. The relative infrequency of tropes can also be explained, at least in part, with reference to the same intentions and cultural influences.

The intention of the vanity poets is basically moral and didactic: the world is untrustworthy and threatens your salvation; therefore renounce it and repent. To make this point, the poets normally concentrated on describing the vileness of the world, quite in the manner of preachers. This, in turn, required a certain amount of realistic description, either of the world's true misery or of its deceptive pleasures. The latter could not be too seductive, and the former had to be convincing. In either case, the poets preferred a factual approach, a tone of utter sobriety and accuracy, in which tropes could be used locally to stress a point, but not in profusion throughout. Even when miniature allegories are the main principles of order, they are developed in a matter-of-fact way from figurative axioms. This rareness of tropes complements the prevalence of symbolic metonymy and literal language. If it is true, as Winifred Nowottny and common sense argue, that the description of sensory experience and private emotions especially calls for metaphor,[28] then we have come a long way towards understanding why there are so few tropes in these poems: sensory and affective details are used here only to fortify general truths, never as poetic subjects per se. And moral, devotional, or pious arguments can be stated explicitly, without tropes.

For contrast, we need only think of the rich figurative language in poetic traditions like symbolism and imagism, which were based largely on sensory and emotional experience. The function of a metaphor is, after all, to describe something unfamiliar in familiar terms: "Since metaphor uses terms in a transferred sense, this means that, subject to some not very serious limitations, a poet who wants to write about object X but finds its terminology defective or resistant to manipulation, can simply move over into the terminology of Y."[29] But the themes of *vanitas*, courtly love, and Christ's Passion were not unfamiliar, and their terminologies were neither defective nor recalcitrant.

The feast songs and Christmas carols also had little need of tropes, though for slightly different reasons. As I have explained, paradox is derived from the nature of Christ, as are symbolic titles such as Christ the King, the Way, the Word, and so on. Otherwise, however, these poems are strikingly poor in figurative language because, by and large, they are not "about" anything; they are not discursive.[30] Metaphor, according to Aristotle, for one, is a means of discovering or delineating truth and therefore presupposes a subject of investigation, in some sense. But the celebratory poems either flatly recite a very well known story, whose details are firmly fixed by the New Testament and tradition, or they exhort the listeners to enjoy themselves, sometimes describing the feast by naming its parts. They do not use feasts or the Christmas events metaphorically. Neither do these poems talk about sensory or emotional reality, though they usually involve both. Thus there is little use for tropes, except occasionally to heighten a description. Even the traditional epithets for Christ and the Virgin are not primarily tropes but etymologies of the proper names.[31] Finally, it is important that these poems were songs, often accompanied by music; the effort of following dense figurative language would have distracted listeners from the total effect.

By their nature and function, the poems are well suited to neutral language. This does not explain the sparseness of figures and subtle connotations; conceivably poems could be written that perform the same functions evocatively, with abundant figures of speech. Within the context of medieval culture, however, the form and the function of these poems are congruent with each other and presumably with other cultural forms, although their exact relation to painting or sculpture, for example, is beyond the scope of this study.

4. The Three Levels of Style

he style of a poem is analogous to the atmosphere of a place, if we remember that poems are more intentional than places. If style is "a characteristic manner of expression" (Abrams, p. 94), then the prevailing style of Middle English poetry is impersonal, down-to-earth, general, and practical. That is, style can be described in nearly the same terms I have already used to describe words and metaphor. It varies mainly with the diction, which varies according to the poet's intention. But the level of style should be discussed in its own right because it colors whole poems, not just words or phrases, and because it can be analyzed into three fairly distinct categories—low, middle, and high—each with distinct uses. These three levels, however different they may be in their origins and effects, are all more or less popular, never esoteric; they are *relatively* low, middle, and high.

Because nearly all the short poems are written in a single poetic language, whose "grammar" I am describing in this study, the differences among levels of style are essentially semantic. I do not find it useful to speak as if style and meaning were separate entities, combined in particular poems with varying degrees of skill. The poet finds his meaning by finding his style, his words, which, after all, comprise his meaning. I will use only one ultimate term, "total meaning," which includes tone, diction, and the rest, rather than two terms such as "meaning" and "style." In this way I can avoid speaking as if one style were "better suited" to expressing idealistic attitudes, and another style "better suited" to a materialistic view of reality. The style *is* the attitude, just as it *is* the denotative meaning and everything else one can understand from the words. To say otherwise is to say that "fresh roses" is a good phrase for dealing with pleasant experience, whereas "rotting corpses" is better suited to conveying unpleasant experience. It is much simpler to say that the two phrases mean different things.

I shall define the three levels of medieval style, then, as a function of verbal meaning, and try to keep them distinct from the three classical levels of style. But although there is not, to my knowledge, any documented connection between the anonymous Middle English poems and

74

the earlier doctrine of the three styles, medieval poets did have an atrophied classical tradition at their disposal. A few historical remarks are therefore in order.

Among the classical sources for medieval rhetoric, the *Ad Herennium* has an especially compact definition of the three styles:

> There are, then, three kinds of style, called types, to which discourse, if faultless, confines itself: the first we call the Grand; the second, the Middle; the third, the Simple. The Grand type consists of a smooth and ornate arrangement of impressive words. The Middle type consists of words of a lower, yet not of the lowest and most colloquial, class of words. The Simple type is brought down even to the most current idiom of standard speech.[1]

The corresponding passage from Geoffroi de Vinsauf's *Documentum de Arte Versificandi* reads:

> There are, then, three styles: low, middle, grand. And the styles are given these names according to the persons or things we are talking about. For when we talk about persons or things of general importance, then the style is grand; about low subjects, it is low; about middling subjects, it is middle. Virgil makes use of each style: low in the *Bucolics*, middle in the *Georgics*, grand in the *Aeneid*.[2]

The classical definition is wholly verbal; it deals with the choice and arrangement of words. The medieval definition is social, in a rather simpleminded way: we use fine language on fine subjects. This confirms the judgment of Rossell Hope Robbins that "the poets who wrote at the request of some nobleman introduced a Latinized or 'aureate' vocabulary, in an effort to create a 'noble' style for their 'noble' readers" (apropos of the Aureate Collections, a group of very expensive manuscripts—14/15th: p. xxiii). When the English poets were conscious of style at all, they must have fit it into some such framework of social decorum. The grandest poems were for God and His Mother— or the poet's mistress—and the lowest were for man the sinner, born and dead in corruption.

Low Style

The terms *colloquial* and *familiar* are both misleading, and *plain* is too mild, so I have settled on the pejorative but accurate term *low* to describe the first level of style. To some extent, the level of a poem's style depends on its particular intention; but even so, there are broad similarities of style in *contemptus* poems, Christmas carols, drinking songs, love lyrics, and others. All are direct and physical, sometimes vulgar, obscene, or boorishly good-humored. The atmosphere of these poems has been well described by Charles Muscatine in connection with medieval bourgeois literature:

> The literature of the bourgeois tradition is "realistic" or "naturalistic," but it neither attempts nor achieves the reportorial detail of the modern fiction describable by these labels. . . . [it has] a remarkable preoccupation with the animal facts of life. . . . the literature at its best gives the impression of dealing with life directly, with something of life's natural shape and vitality.[3]

Among *contemptus* poems, the low style is usually colored by graphic images of death, decay, old age, and other tokens of mortality. These poems, in their themes, functions, and style, resemble Anglo-Saxon gnomes, riddles, and assorted types of practical verse. I do not know of any direct historical link, but the Middle English verses are similarly earthy and epigrammatic; there is certainly a generic if not a historical relationship (see p. 132). For example:

Wrecche mon, wy artou proud,
þat art of herth I-maked?
hydyr ne browtestou no schroud,°   *clothing*
4   but pore þou come & naked.
Wen þi soule is faren° out,   *passed*
þi body with erthe y-raked,
þat body þat was so ronk° and loud,   *rank, haughty*
8   Of alle-men is i-hated.

There are many other such epigrams (see pp. 111, 113, and 121) which are knit together with tightly reasoned didacticism, especially from the earlier Middle English period; but longer poems set in a low style are also prominent, as are poems which include low elements or passages.

Certain drinking songs and Christmas carols have as much physicality as the *contemptus* poems, but its effect is quite different. In one Advent carol, for instance, the details are often unlovely, and the language is colloquial and comically abusive:

2

While thou [Advent] haste be within oure howse
We ete no puddynges ne no sowce,
But stynking fisshe not worthe a lowce;
    Farewele [fro vs both alle and sume.]

76

4

Thou has vs fedde with plaices thynne,
Nothing on them but bone and skynne;
Therefore oure loue thou shalt not wynne;
    Farewele [fro vs both alle and sume.]

5

With muskilles gaping afture the mone
Thou hast vs fedde at nyght and none,
But ones a wyke, and that to sone;
    Farewele [fro vs both alle and sume.]

6

Oure brede was browne, oure ale was thynne,
Oure brede was musty in the bynne,
Oure ale soure or° we did begynne;   ere
    Fare[wele fro vs both alle and sume.]

11

Thou maist not dwelle with none eastate;
Therfore with vs thou playest chekmate.
Go hens, or we will breke thy pate!
    Farewele [fro vs both alle and sume.]

                              (C:3)

Even the best kinds of food mentioned are not gourmet items, and the
colorful turns of phrase in stanza 2, line 3, and stanza 11, line 3, are
well suited to the familiar "thou." Poems of direct address especially
lend themselves to this kind of phrasing:

	I am so dry I can-not spek,	
12	I am nygh choked with my mete—	
	I trow° þe butler be a-slepe.	believe
	with how, butler, how! bevis a towght!	drink to all (?)
	ffill þe boll, butler, [& let þe cup rowght!°]	move around
16	Butler, butler, ffill þe boll,	
	or elles I beshrewe thy noll!°	head
	I trow we must þe bell toll.	
	with how, butler, how! bevis a towght!	
20	ffill þe boll, [butler, & let þe cup rowght!]	
	Iff þe butlers name be water,°	(pun on "Walter")
	I wold he were a galow-claper,°	gallows-bird
	but if° he bryng vs drynk þe raþer°	unless; more quickly
24	with how, butler, how! bevis a towght!	
	ffill [þe boll, butler, & let þe cup rowght]	

                    (14/15th:14)

In general, the tone of such poems is homely, boisterous, and crudely good-natured; and the themes are the simple joys of eating and drinking, with or without reference to religious occasions.

There are a good many popular love songs in a similar vein; the famous "De Clerico et Puella" has low phrasing, especially in the "puella's" speeches ("be stille, þou fol, y calle þe riht; cost [canst] þou neuer blynne [stop]?' "); and the satires lend themselves to reasonably coarse language:

> how! hey! it is non les,°   *no lie*
> I dar not seyȝ quan che seyȝt "pes!"[1]
>
> ȝyng men, I warne ȝou euerychon:
> Elde wywys tak ȝe non;
> for I my-self haue on° at hom—   *one*
> 4   I dar not seyn quan che seyȝt "pes!"
>
> Quan I cum fro þe plow at non,
> In a reuen° dych myn mete is don;   *riven, cracked*
> I dar not askyn our dame a spon—
> 8   I dar not [seyn quan che seyȝt "pes!"]
>
> If I aske our dame bred,
> che takyt a staf & brekit myn hed,
> & doþ me rennyn vnder þe bed—
> 12   I dar not [seyn quan che seyȝt "pes!"]
>
> If I aske our dame fleych,
> che brekit myn hed with a dych:
> "boy, þou art not worȝt a reych!"°   *rush*
> 16   I dar [not seyn quan che seyȝt "pes!"]
>
> If I aske our dame chese,
> "boy," che seyȝt, al at ese,
> "þou art not worȝt half a pese."
> 20   I dar not sey quan che seyȝt "pes!"

Whatever the specific purpose of the poem, the low style creates a sense of forthright intimacy, usually between speaker and audience.

High Style

At the opposite end of the scale is the high style, which is polite and ethereal where its opposite is gross. In the medieval high style, as

---

[1] *I dare not speak when she says "peace!"*

it appears in romances, the "setting, landscape, and paraphernalia . . . tend to be exotic, superlative in quality and economy, and, in the best poetry, generating a meaning by their presence without regard for their practical utility in the action. . . ."[4] Two very important foreign influences, one French and the other Latin, have colored this level of style: courtly and aureate diction.

Courtly diction can easily be used in small quantities, like a powerful dye; for this reason it sometimes adds its upper-class tone to poems of a distinctly popular sort. In this case the effect is, of course, ironical. For instance, in the *contemptus* poems, courtly diction is usually a means of stressing the irony in the truth that all mortal beauty, all the *gloria mundi*, must perish—not only perish, but suffer the humiliation of rotting:

Wen þe turuf is þi tuur,°	*tower*	
& þe put° is þi bour,	*pit*	
þi wel° & þi wite° þrote	*skin; white*	
4 ssulen wormes to note.	*shall be of use to worms*	
Wat helpit þe þenne		
al þe worilde wnne?	*all the world's pleasure*	

The courtly elements, clichés taken from the poetry of graceful compliment, are "þi tuur," "þi bour," and "þi wite þrote." By juxtaposing them with the turf, the pit, and the usual gnawing worms, the poet has created a piece of obvious but effective irony, rather like a simple woodcut. He has only to name a few key words, and the whole world of courtly love, with all its precarious grace, is present to the mind's eye—only to shrivel from contact with burrowing worms and cold earth.

The tone of this epigram is grimly material, even despairing. But the usual effect of courtly diction in the poems of tragedy is to cast a gentle, elegiac mood over the facts of death and decay, not falsifying the situation but making it poignant rather than grossly shocking. This effect is strengthened by the use of such commonplaces as the *ubi sunt*, descriptions of mortal beauty, or by rare dignity of phrasing. These techniques suggest the general character of a high-style poem: it is on the one hand formal and elegiac, gently mourning the glorious past, while on the other hand it describes present reality *sub specie aeternitatis*. In both cases only beautiful, idealized details are admitted. These graceful laments are very similar in mood to Anglo-

Saxon poems such as "The Ruin" and "The Wanderer" and to the elegiac passages in *Beowulf*. The Middle English lyrics normally put more emphasis on the penitential theme, but they have the same lofty sadness as the Anglo-Saxon, the same palpable sense of worldly delights long past—goblets of wine or mead, brave comrades, beautiful women, splendid dwelling places:

> Where are the horses gone to? Where are the men gone? Where
> are the givers of treasures gone?
> Where are the places of feasting gone? Where are the joys of the hall?
> Alas, the bright cup! Alas, the armed warrior!
> 95 Alas, the prince's glory! How that time has passed,
> Gone under night-helm, as though it had never been!
>
> . . . .
>
> All is hardship in the kingdom of the earth;
> the workings of fate change this world under heaven.
> Here goods are only lent us, here friends are only lent,
> here men are only lent, here women are only lent us;
> 110 all this earthen foundation becomes empty.

> *Hwaer cwom mearg? Hwaer cwom mago? Hwaer cwom maþþumgyfa?*
> *Hwaer cwom symbla gesetu? Hwaer sindon seledreamas?*
> *Eala beorht buna! Eala byrnwiga!*
> 95 *Eala þeodnes þrym! Hu seo þrag gewat,*
> *genap under nihthelm, swa heo no waere.*
>
> . . . .
>
> *Eall is earfoðlic eorþan rice,*
> *onwendeþ wyrda gesceaft weoruld under heofonum.*
> *Her bið feoh laene, her bið freond laene,*
> *her bið mon laene, her bið maeg laene,*
> 110 *eal þis eorþan gesteal idel weorþeð!*[5]

French diction is, however, most prominent in the courtly love poems, which are normally written in a high style. One would expect the English translator of Charles d'Orléans to use French words,[6] especially in rhymes, where French suffixes are so convenient (gouernans, plesans, obeyssance, repentance, greuance); but the same French diction may be found in anonymous courtly poems:

> O mestres, whye
> Owtecaste am I
> all vtterly

4	from your pleasaunce?	
	Sythe ye & I	
	or° thys, truly,	*ere*
	famyliarly	
8	haue had pastaunce.°	*diversion, pleasure*
	And lovyngly	
	ye wolde aply	
	þy company	
12	to my comforte;	
	But now, truly,	
	vnlovyngly	
	ye do deny	
16	Me to resorte.°	*"resort" (to you)*
	And me to see	
	as strange° ye be,	*aloof, distant*
	as thowe þat ye	
20	shuld nowe deny,	
	or else possesse	
	þat nobylnes	
	To be dochess	
24	of grete Savoy.	
	But sythe þat ye	
	So strange wylbe	
	As toward me,	
28	& wyll not medyll,°	*"meddle," have to do (with me)*
	I truste, percase,°	*perhaps*
	to fynde some grace	
	to haue free chayse,°	*hunting (of other women)*
32	& spede° as welle!	*succeed*

Although these words bring their own graceful, slightly exotic connotations into English verse, they are elegant mainly because they refer to elegant things, just as French *dinner* is a more distinguished meal than English *breakfast*.[7] But even at its most Gallic and refined, the tone of Middle English poems never approaches the rarified elegance of some modern verse:

> And light
> That fosters seraphim and is to them
> Coiffeur of haloes, fecund jeweller—
> Was the sun concoct for angels or for men?[8]

Aureate diction, which has been more thoroughly studied than other aspects of Middle English diction,[9] also raises the style of many anonymous poems, especially devotional poems of praise. There are many examples of jewel-encrusted praise for the Virgin Mary, and indeed for earthly ladies, but one is enough:

Tota pulcra° and principall	*wholly beautiful*
of plente that is plenitude,	
Castell of clennes, I hyr call,	
4 that beldith° in beatitude,	*dwells*
beyng as clene as clere crystall	
Whose meuynge° is mansuetude.°	*prompting, desire; gentleness*
hyr sete° is sett sempeternall	*seat*
8 In excelsis so celsitude.	*In the highest loftiness (?)*

(15th:45)

The heavy Latin nearly crowds the English out of the lines, as it actually does in macaronic poems. The Latin words in this Marian lyric have not been assimilated to English; one feels them to be foreign, strained, and very formal, like many of the classical Latin words imported into English during and since the Renaissance.[10] The result is a stilted high style, the very opposite of down-to-earth, idiomatic writing. This effect is greatly enhanced, once again, by the meanings of the words, which were felt to be inherently lofty and attractive: clennes, beatitude, clere crystall, mansuetude, in excelsis, celsitude.

A high style is naturally one of the requisites for religious poems of celebration. Christmas songs and carols are often filled with emblematic praise for Christ or the Virgin; they tend to have a strong theological emphasis; and at best they give a rare sense of wonder and sublimity. The burden of one famous carol has a sensuous-theological pun on "vertu" as "strength or fragrance" and "virtue" in the modern sense:

[T]her [is n]o rose of swych° vertu	*such*
As is the rose that bare Jhesu.	

1

Ther is no ro[se of] swych vertu
As is the rose that bar Jhesu;
Alleluya.

2

For in this rose conteynyd was
Heuen and erthe in lytyl space,
   Res miranda.   *a marvelous thing*

3

Be° that rose we may weel see   *By*
That he is God in personys thre,
   Pari forma.   *in equal form*

4

The aungelys sungyn the sheperdes to:
'Gloria in excelcis Deo.'   *"Glory to God in the highest"*
   Gaudeamus.   *Let us rejoice*

5

[L]eue we al this wordly merthe,
And folwe we this joyful berthe;
   Transeamus.   *Let us pass on*

The same carol celebrates the mysteries of the Incarnation (stanza 2) and the Trinity (stanza 3). And the famous "I syng of a myden" is not only built on a flawlessly apt metaphor—the coming of the Holy Spirit to Mary is as imperceptible, refreshing, and total as the spreading of dew upwards from grass to flower to branches—it is also compounded of natural details that we still find lovely in themselves:[11]

I syng a of a myden þat is makeles

I syng of a myden þat is makeles,°   *peerless, mateless*
kyng of alle kynges to here sone che ches.°   *chose*

he cam also stylle° þer his moder was   *as silently*
4 as dew in aprylle, þat fallyt on þe gras.

he cam also stylle to his moderes bowr
as dew in aprille, þat fallyt on þe flour.

he cam also stylle þer his moder lay
8 as dew in aprille, þat fallyt on þe spray.°   *twigs*

moder & mayden was neuer non but che—
wel may swych a lady godes moder be.

These Christmas poems are no less "high" than the poems of praise or *vanitas* that I have discussed; but their affective coloration is naturally quite different.

Middle Style

I have chosen the obvious term *middle* to cover the broad range between low and high, the two extremes on the scale. This is simply to say that not all the poems are clearly low or high. The middle style, then, must be defined negatively: it excludes the distinctive marks of the two more noticeable styles. It is not shockingly realistic, idiomatic, coarsely good-humored, aureate, Frenchified, or gently elegiac. Poems in the middle style are usually made of straightforward statements, often explanatory and rarely eccentric. Some typical examples are "Spende, and god schal sende" (p. 65), "By thys fyre I warme my handys" (p. 95), and this mild admonition:

Euen,° it es a richʒ ture°—	*Heaven; tower*
wele bies im þat itte may win—	*well be him that may win it*
of Mirthes ma° þan ert° may think	*more; art*
4 and þa iois sal neuer blin.°	*cease*
Sinful man, bot þu þe mend	*unless you mend yourself*
and for-sak þin wikkid sin,	
þu mon° singge hay, 'wailaway!'°	*may; (exclamation of despair)*
8 for comes þu neuer mare þar-I[nne].	

It should be apparent that the three levels of Middle English style are not the same as the three classical levels, in spite of strong resemblances. The medieval low style, like its classical counterpart, is often didactic and logical, and the high style, also like the classical, eschews coarseness; but the whole center of gravity in medieval short poems is lower than in classical Latin. Even the loftier poems are didactic and plain in comparison to the Virgilian grand style. And the classical styles are arranged on a scale of emotional intensity: the grand style was expected to be overpowering, the low style subdued, and the middle style merely pleasing. The Middle English low style, however, is often more emotionally powerful than its opposite, and the middle style is not conspicuously pleasing.

The level of style, as a function of words and syntax, necessarily reflects the public nature of Middle English short poems. One can see this reflection most distinctly in contrast with Latin and modern English poetry: the medieval poem does not achieve or attempt the grandness of classical Latin, as exemplified by much of the *Aeneid*, or the refined elegance and irony of such moderns as Stevens, Ransom, or Wilbur. Unlike these men, the medieval poet was not writing for a select audience with a high degree of literary culture. There were no Roman aristocrats or American literary critics in the Middle Ages. Medieval poets had to write in simple styles because their verses dealt with general themes and situations, and were meant to be understood at one hearing.

5. Sound and Rhythm

he previous chapter deals mostly with the smallest elements in the poems, words and phrases, without much consideration of how they fit together. But in any poem, there are large and small devices for relating these parts: assonance may link two or three words in a line, and some form of logic may give shape to a whole poem of fifty or a hundred lines. Under "sound and rhythm" I have grouped those aural and syntactic principles that connect words, phrases, and lines: sound devices (alliteration, assonance), meter, and various kinds of relationship between syntax and rhythmic pauses (syntax and lines, syntax and caesuras, couplets and rhyme, pairs of words, hypotaxis and parataxis, repetition, parallel constructions). All of these principles may be combined, but it is simpler to treat them separately, without trying to map out the countless ways in which rhyme can modify alliteration or meter can interact with parallel constructions, and so forth. It is, in fact, impossible not to deal with these interrelationships, but I shall only do so incidentally.

Figures of Sound

The most important figures of sound in the Middle English lyrics are assonance and alliteration, especially the latter. Their main purpose is to bind words together emphatically, not to point out symbolic affinities between sound and sense; the poets had to keep in mind the limits of their audience. This led the poet to simplify his verse—more specifically, to use figures of sound in the interests of clarity—which led in turn to the use of very few devices for echoic stressing of the sense. Anyone who has attended poetry readings knows how ill-suited most well written modern poetry is to public recitation; the verse is too highly wrought for the audience to get more than a small fraction of its full meaning. Among medieval audiences, the ratio of understanding to bafflement was certainly much higher.

The Middle English poem most celebrated for its sound-texture is probably "Alysoun," from the manuscript Harley 2253 (p. 22), in which alliteration and assonance are especially prominent:

> On heu hire *her* is *fayr* ynoh,
> hire *browe broune*, hir *eʒe* blake,
> Wiþ lossum *chere* he on *me* loh;
> wiþ middel *smal* & wel *ymake*.
>
> . . . .
>
> Nihtes *when* y *wende* & wake—
> for-þi myn *wonges* waxeþ *won*—
> leudi, al for þine sake,
> *longinge* is ylent me *on*.
>
> (13th:77)

(I have indicated only the assonance, since the alliteration and rhymes are quite obvious.) Both figures of sound tend to link pairs of words and to coincide with heavy metrical stresses. The effect is thus all the more emphatic, to the great convenience of anyone hearing the poem for the first time. But there is no intrinsic, suggestive relationship among the meanings of the words thus linked: "when" and "wende" are related only by sound, and not even "browe" and "broune," or "her" and "fayr," have a tract of common meaning which the echoed sounds could intensify. Brownness and brows are related by syntax, not by inherent similarity. It may be helpful to contrast this thirteenth-century poem with a passage from Yvor Winters' "On a View of Pasadena from the Hills":

> The hills
> Lie naked but not light. The darkness spills
> Down the remoter gulleys; pooled, will stay
> Too low to melt, not yet alive with day.
> Below the windows, the lawn, matted deep
> Under its close-cropped tips with dewy sleep,
> Gives off a faint hush, all its plushy swarm
> Alive with coolness reaching to be warm.[1]

The relations between sound and sense in these lines are extremely complex. The most important sounds are the liquids, especially *l*, the back vowels ($\bar{u}$, $\bar{o}$), and the voiceless fricative *sh*. The poet's general method is to use these sounds to relate words whose meanings are intrinsically relatable. In this way the resemblances in sound suggest or activate the possible resemblances in meaning, and the resulting complex of sound and meaning is very strong and subtle. Thus the darkness of the hills and gulleys is associated with the liquid *l* and with actual cool liquid: "The darkness spills . . . [and] pooled, will stay / Too low to melt." The back vowels in these lines ("pooled," "Too low") prepare the transition to the domestic scene by way of "win*dows*" and "*close*-cropped tips" (ll. 7–8) to the "*cool*ness" in line 10; the cool, liquid darkness of the hills is transferred by association to the grass, just as the potential brightness of the dark hills ("not yet alive with day," l. 6) is echoed in the potential warmth of the cool, moist grass ("alive with coolness," l. 10). One senses the impending sun, which will "perfect" both hills and grass. Finally, the sibilants and back vowels in "faint *hush*" and "*plush*y swarm" (l. 9) suggest the tactile-aural experience of walking on firm, close-cropped grass heavy with dew.

Not only "Alysoun," but even the most aurally mimetic poem in Middle English is a far less rich complex of sounds and meaning than the Winters passage. This heavily alliterative complaint against black-smiths does suggest the din of a medieval smithy, sometimes with explicit onomatopoeia, as in lines 6 and 19:

> Swarte smekyd smeþes, smateryd wyth smoke,[1]
> dryue me to deth wyth den[2] of here dyntes![3]
> Swech noys on nyghtes ne herd men neuer:
> 4 What knauene[4] cry, & clateryng of knockes!
> þe cammede[5] kongons[6] cryen after "col,[7] col!"
> & blowen here bellewys þat al here brayn brestes.
> "huf, puf!" seyth þat on. "haf, paf!" þat oþer.
> 8 þei spyttyn & spraulyn & spellyn[8] many spelles,[9]
> þei gnauen[1] & gnacchen,[2] þei gronys togydere,
> and holdyn hem[3] hote wyth here hard hamers.
> of a bole[4] hyde ben here barm-fellys,[5]
> 12 here schankes ben schakeled for þe fere-flunderys;[6]

[1] *Black-smoked smiths, besmirched with smoke*
[2] *din*
[3] *blows*
[4] *of workmen*
[5] *snub-nosed(?), crooked*
[6] *changelings*
[7] *coal*
[8] *tell*
[9] *tales*

[1] *gnaw*
[2] *gnash*
[3] *themselves*
[4] *bull's*
[5] *leather aprons*
[6] *their legs are protected against the sparks*

heuy hamerys þei han þat hard ben handled,
stark strokes þei stryken on a stelyd[7] stokke.[8]
"lus, bus! las, das!" rowtyn be rowe—[9]
16 sweche dolful a dreme þe deuyl it todryue;[1]
þe mayster longith a lityl & lascheth a lesse,[2]
twyneth hem tweyn, and towchith a treble.[3]
"tik, tak! hic, hac! tiket, taket! tyk, tak!
20 lus, bus! lus, das!"—swych lyf þei ledyn!
Alle cloþemerys[4] cryst hem gyue sorwe,
may no man for brenwaterys[5] on nyght han hys rest!

Unlike the figures of sound in "Alysoun," these are meant to evoke
what is being described. But unlike the lines by Winters, the black-
smith poem is simple in its structural use of sounds: the alliteration
and onomatopeia affect only the lines in which they occur; they do not
play lightly back and forth over the lines like overtones, connecting
themes and motifs. I do not mean to suggest that the medieval poet
tried to write like a modern and failed. On the contrary, Winters would
have failed if he had written for a listening rather than a reading public: his effects are too subtle. The authors of "Swarte smeked smeþes,"
"Alysoun," and other medieval poems accomplished their particular,
unsubtle purposes.

A similar though less important figure of sound in these lyrics is
the wordplay. It resembles the other medieval sound figures in that its
use is restricted to single lines or phrases; it does not coordinate parts
of the poem. And it draws the listener's attention to the *significatio* of
the line. Speaking of the lost state of mankind before the birth of
Christ, a poet can use assonance to suggest the familiar anagram
AVE/EVA: "With *aue* it went a-way" (13th:17B, l. 23). Here the phonetic resemblance between "aue" and "a-way" points to the efficacy of
"Ave" in putting sin away. The same kind of logical, aural wordplay
can be found in these lines from another thirteenth-century poem:

[7] *steel*
[8] *anvil*
[9] *(they) crash in turn*
[1] *may the devil drive away such a doleful racket*
[2] *the master lengthens a small piece (of metal) and hammers a smaller one*
[3] *twines them both together and strikes a treble note (with his hammer) (?)*
[4] *horse-armorers*
[5] *water-burners, blacksmiths, who "burn" water with hot iron*

Al þat ioye is went away,
þat *wele is* comen te *weylaway*

. . . .

And þenk on him þat þereonne ȝaf
His *lif* þat wes so *lef.*°   *dear*
(13th:48)

The italicized words in each couplet are bound together with striking
effect: just as "wele" becomes "weylaway" by adding a suffix, so does
earthly "wele" become eternal "weylaway" by persisting in sin; and
the mere lowering of the vowel from "lif" to "lef" stresses the near-
identity of these two words in sound and sense. Such effects are striking, but not so subtle as to elude the ear.

Meter

Corrupt manuscripts often make it impossible to discern the poet's
exact metrical intention, but all of the poems are at least roughly ac-
centual, with varying numbers of slack syllables and varying numbers
of feet per line (usually four, often five).[2] The metrical stress is heavy,
and it usually coincides with the rhetorical stress. All of this means
that the meter, like the figures of sound, is not capable of truly subtle
effects; the metrical norm is so vaguely defined—it allows such large
variation in the number of syllables per line, stressed and unstressed
alike—that small variations are imperceptible.* The poet cannot use
a trochaic substitution or an inverted foot to good effect, because in
most poems a foot may be trochaic, inverted, or nearly anything else
at random.

A good specimen of Middle English meter, though perhaps more
regular than usual, is the following:

What is this worlde but oonly vanyte?
Who trustith fortune sonnest hath a falle.
Ech man tak heed of prodigalite,
4   Welth that is past no man agayn may calle.
The grenowst° wounde þat euer man had or schalle   *greenest*

Is to thynk on welth þat is gon and past,
And in olde age in mysery to be cast.

* For this discussion, among many other things, I am indebted to Yvor Winters'
teaching and writings (see *In Defense of Reason*, especially pp. 103–150).

90

The metrical norm is clearly iambic pentameter, but the alternation of stressed and unstressed syllables serves only to distribute the heavy accents among rhetorically significant words. The poet does not grade the level of stress or invert a foot for special effect, and I see no good reason why the sixth line should have only four main stresses ("Is to thýnk on wélth þat is gón and pást"). The meter is far less tightly logical in "What is this worlde" than in the following epigram by Catherine Davis:

> In solitude, my thoughts hell-bent will flow,
> But speech, breakwater, checks them as they go:
> Converse with me—they reach you tame and slow.[3]

In this this poem, where every syllable is accounted for, the meter carefully underlines the sense. The first line is regular, although the fourth foot is extremely heavy for the sake of emphasis. The second line, however, introduces a sharp irregularity, an inversion in the second foot, which rhythmically suggests a breakwater meeting the impact of a wave, and thus greatly enhances the metaphoric sense of speech as a breakwater for thoughts. The last line is perfectly regular, as befits the movement of thoughts after they have struck the "break-water"—they are now "tame and slow." This degree of metrical subtlety is, in a certain sense, too sophisticated for the anonymous medieval poets. They normally used meter, as they used figures of sound, to outline the broad contours of their meaning, because their meaning had *only* broad contours. They were interested in seducing women, marking the seasons of the year, preventing books from being stolen, drinking convivially, gaining the favor of Christ and Mary, avoiding hell, and other matters more directly useful than understanding how one complicated poet uses speech to check her hell-bent thoughts.

In one kind of Middle English poem, however, the meter may be sensitive enough to indicate fine degrees of stress: in songs, especially those with short lines. But Stephen Manning, who considers the Middle English short poems primarily as songs,[4] argues rightly that "the contents of a song lyric are often . . . colorless, and the sound pattern must create, practically of itself, the poet's emotional or imaginative intensity" (Manning, p. 11). In other words, even when the meter is finely modulated, it does not qualify the meaning as precisely as does the meter of the Davis epigram, because the meaning itself is so slight. Since there is little to be qualified, the meter can accomplish little; it is like a fine arabesque around the edge of a very simple manuscript illumination. Two cases in point are "O mestres, whye" (p. 80) and this thirteenth-century Marian lyric:

Of on þat is so fayr and briȝt
    velud maris stella,   *like the star of the sea*
Briȝter þan þe day-is liȝt,
4   *parens & puella,*   *parent and maiden*
Ic crie to þe, þou se to me,
Leuedy, preye þi sone for me
    tam pia,   *so pious, devoted*
8 þat ic mote° come to þe,   *may*
    maria.

Of kare° conseil þou ert best,   *care, misery*
    felix fecundata;   *happy and fruitful one*
12 Of alle wery þou ert rest,
    mater honorata.   *honored mother*
Bi-sek him wit milde mod
þat for ous alle sad is blod   *shed his blood*
16 *in cruce,*   *on the cross*
þat we moten° komen til him   *may*
    In luce.   *in the light*

Al þis world was for-lore
20 *eua peccatrice*   *through Eve the sinner*
Tyl our lord was y-bore
    de te genitrice;   *of you, the mother*
With *aue* it went a-way,
24 þuster° nyth and comet þe day   *dark*
    salutis,   *of salvation, health*
þe welle springet hut° of þe   *out*
    uirtutis.   *of virtue*

28 Leuedi, flour of alle þing,
    rosa sine spina,   *rose without thorn*
þu bere ihesu, heuene-king,
    gratia diuina.   *by divine grace*
32 Of alle þu berst þe pris,
Leuedi, quene of parays°   *paradise*
    electa,   *chosen*
Mayde milde Moder *es*   *Gentle maid, you are*
36 *effecta*   *made a mother*

<table>
<tr><td>

Wel he wot° he is þi sone
  uentre quem portasti;
He wyl nout werne þe þi bone
40 paruum quem lactasti.
So hende° and so god he his,
He hauet brout° ous to blis
  superni;
44 Þat hauet hi-dut þe foule put
  inferni.

</td><td>

knows
whom you carried in your womb
He will not refuse you your request,
He whom you suckled as a baby
gracious
brought
of heaven
That has shut the foul pit
of hell

</td></tr>
</table>

Most of the metrical interest of these poems lies in the relationships among syntax, meter, and line-breaks. Songs preserved with music, such as the famous "Svmer is icumen in,"* "Mirie it is while sumer ilast" (p. 116), and many of the fifteenth-century carols, are also metrically quite regular, with strong accents falling at even intervals on the most significant words. To avoid the possible monotony of alternate stressed and unstressed syllables, the poet could vary the length of the lines, to help convey, for example, a strong sense of reciprocity, as in the last four lines of this song:

<table>
<tr><td>

Tappster, fille Anoþer Ale.
  Anonne have I doo;[1]
god send vs good sale.°
4 Avale° þe stake,° Avale,
  here ys good Ale I-fovnde!
    drynke to me,
      & I to þe,
8 and lette þe coppe goo Rounde.

</td><td>

joy
veil (?); ale-stake outside the tavern

</td></tr>
</table>

* The manuscript also includes careful directions in Latin for singing the upper voices of this four-part *rota:*

<table>
<tr><td>

Svmer is icumen in,
Lhude° sing cuccu!
Groweþ sed and bloweþ med
4 and springþ þe wde° nu.
Sing cuccu!

</td><td>

Spring has arrived
loudly
the seed grows and the meadow blossoms
forest

</td></tr>
<tr><td>

Awe° bleteþ after lomb,
lhouþ after calue cu,
8 Bulluc sterteþ,° bucke uerteþ.°
Murie sing cuccu!
Cuccu, cuccu,
Wel singes þu cuccu.
12 ne swik° þu nauer nu!

</td><td>

ewe
the cow lows after the calf
leaps; farts

cease

</td></tr>
</table>

Sing cuccu nu, Sing cuccu!

Sing cuccu, Sing cuccu nu!

[1] *I have just done it (the tapster's reply)*

Syntax and Versification

Like the metrical pattern, the verse-line in a Middle English poem has a very firm identity. Lines and meter both underscore the primary sense of the words; they serve the interests of plain clarity. The line is an artificial unit based on a metrical count of syllables. It can preserve its typographic identity in the most rampant of free verse, but if its rhythmic identity is to be preserved, the mechanical pause at the end of the line must tend to coincide with a pause in the syntax. It need only "tend to" coincide, because run-on lines do not dissolve into prose unless they are used indiscriminately. The sense of a line either runs on into the next line or it does not; but there are various degrees of pause at the ends of lines. This means that deciding whether specific lines are end-stopped or run-on is a matter of tact and degree, as is the question of how many run-on lines are required to make a "run-on poem." Granting all these reservations, however, I think it is fair to say that in Middle English short poems the sense usually pauses at the line-break, though there are many exceptions to prove the rule. This is to confirm the findings of J. V. Cunningham, among others, who, in an excellent comparative study of classical and medieval-Tudor verse, has concluded that "the [classical] plays the syntactical structure against the metrical line; the [medieval] shows a marked coincidence of the two."[5]

But how does this bear on the general purpose and character of the poems? We must consider that the syntax itself is by and large quite ordinary, and therefore suited, like other features of these poems, to aural and public consumption. It is the kind of syntax that Donald Davie has described as "aesthetically neutral . . . unremarkable, like a human frame that is neither close-knit nor loose-limbed, neither well- nor ill-proportioned, but just normal."[6] Again there are exceptions, some of which I shall discuss later, but in general the syntax gives the impression of someone speaking normally, without trying for special effects through dislocated word order (except to make rhymes!) or even through complicated hypotaxis. If neither the figures of sound, the meter, nor the syntax is very highly wrought, the poet must, then, do something else in order to make stylistic use of the rhythmic, auditory texture of his verse. Otherwise a whole broad range of stylistic potential will remain inert, a dead weight on the meaning.

What the poet does is to provide most of his lines with syntactic frames. When we read "By thys fyre I warme my handys" and the rest, we have a strong, palpable sense of things and actions, because each main word acquires deliberateness from the syntax:

Januar	By thys fyre I warme my handys;
Februar	And with my spade I delfe my landys.
Marche	Here I sette my thynge to sprynge;
4 Aprile	And here I here the fowlis synge.
Maij	I am as lyght as byrde in bowe;
Junij	And I wede my corne well I-now.
Julij	With my sythe my mede I mawe;
8 Auguste	And here I shere my corne full lowe.
September	With my flayll I erne my brede;
October	And here I sawe my whete so rede.
November	At Martynesmasse I kylle my swyne;
12 December	And at Cristesmasse I drynke redde wyne.

Thus the relationship between syntax and line, like the heavy, simple meter, reinforces the plain meaning of the words.

Sometimes the break in line and syntax is made even sharper by a change of language, as in this savage macaronic satire:

ffreers, freers, wo ȝe be!	
ministri malorum.	*ministers of evils*
ffor many a mannes soule brynge ȝe	
4 *ad penas inffernorum.*	*to the tortures of hell*
whan seyntes ffelle ffryst ffrom heuen,	
quo prius habitabant,	*where they had lived before*
In erthe leyftt þo synnus vij	
8 *& ffratres communicabant.*[1]	
ffolnes was þe ffryst ffloure	
quem ffratres pertulerunt,	*which the friars brought*
ffor folnes & fals derei°	*violence*
12 *multi perierunt.*	*many perished*

(HP:67)

The sense can afford to run on somewhat from the third to the fourth line, since the change to Latin is sufficiently abrupt. And forty-two such lines, mostly end-stopped and partly in goliardic meter, are as emphatic as any poem needs to be; no one could have mistaken the sense.

[1] *and friars partook of them (the sins)*

It is only fair to balance this extreme with the other, more exceptional extreme. Though they are not common, run-ons can be used for clear stylistic purposes, especially in short-lined songs:

Querela diuina   *divine complaint*
O man vnkynde° / hafe in mynde   *unkind, unnatural*
  My paynes smert!
Beholde & see, / Þat is for þe
4   Percyd, my hert.

And ȝitt I wolde, / Or þan þu schuld
  þi saule forsake,
On cros with payne / Scharp deth, agayne
8   ffor þi luf take.

ffor whilk I aske / None oþer taske,
  Bot luf agayne.
Me þan to luf, / Al thyng a-bofe,   *thou ought then to be glad*
12   þow aght be fayne.   *to love me above all things*

    Responsio humana   *human response*
O lord, right dere, / Þi wordes I here
  with hert ful sore;
Þerfore fro synne / I hope to blynne,°   *cease*
16   And grefe no more.

Bot in þis case / Now helpe, þi grace,
  My frelnes;
Þat I may euer / Do þi pleser,
20   With lastyngnes.

Þis grace to gytt, / Þi moder eeke
  Euer be prone,°   *eager, "prone"*
Þat we may alle / In-to þi halle,
24   With ioy, cum sone. Amen.

The run-on from line 3 to line 4 is functional: "Percyd" would in any case draw attention to itself because, as an inverted foot in the first position, it breaks the pattern of the first three lines; but the enjambment throws added weight onto the word. The total effect is to stress the fact and the meaning of the Passion: the suffering of Christ for mankind. The sense of line 3 is suspended briefly after "þe," the final and therefore climactic word; its resolution in "Percyd" is as sharp and forceful as a spear-thrust.

But the usual technique is to stop the sense at the end of the metrical line, and even at measured intervals within the line. The caesura is frequently heavy, and when it is placed according to a deliberate pattern, it tends to recur in the same position from line to line:

> Swete ihesu, king of blisse,
> Min herte loue, min herte lisse,°   *peace, joy*
> Þou art swete mid I-wisse°—   *certainly, with certainty*
> 4   Wo is him þat þe shal misse.
>
> Swete ihesu, min herte liȝt,
> Þou art dai wiþ-houten niȝt,
> Þou ȝeue me strengþe and eke miȝt
> 8   For-to louien þe al riȝt.
>
> Swete ihesu, mi soule bote,°   *cure*
> In min herte þou sette a rote°   *root*
> Of þi loue þat is so swote,°   *sweet*
> 12   And wite hit þat hit springe mote.   *and guide it that it may grow*

In this poem, a caesura occurs in almost every line after the second foot, although the caesuras are lighter in the last lines of the first two stanzas, and there is none at all in the last line of the poem—another case of gaining emphasis by breaking a well established pattern. This poem may be more regular than most, but it is not abnormal. Its extreme symmetry, increased by the monorhyme in each stanza, has the same general purpose as the other traits examined so far in this chapter: it sets up a clear, powerful expectation in the listener, making it easy for him to grasp and remember the verses.

The symmetry of the poems often has a strongly "rectangular" quality: tetrameter lines are divided in half, arranged in quatrains, and linked in couplets. For some obscure reason, even numbers, especially two and four, seem to have more stability than odd numbers; perhaps because buildings, tables, and other solid objects usually have four-sided surfaces. In any case, medieval "numbers" (verses) have something of the blocklike symmetry of New Jerusalem as seen by the Pearl poet. The outlines are not blurred.

Of course the many poems in rhyme royal and ballade stanzas[7] are also symmetrical and distinct in their outlines, but the anonymous, practical poems are usually written in simpler measures—quatrains and couplets—which are even more distinct and "rectangular." In Rossell Hope Robbins' words, "the more practical the lyric, the more simple the form" (14/15th: p. xlviii). Much of what can be said about the simplest of all stanza forms, the couplet, can also be said about the Middle English quatrain. Since the medieval poets, unlike Dryden and Pope, did not perfect the art of the couplet, they left it very little differentiated from the quatrain. Both forms serve to connect words and lines and to intensify the already strong sense of structural definition. The couplet, at least, often has as much unity as the line, as it does in this lyric with its sharp rhymes and climactic third couplet:

> God wiht hise aungeles i haue for-loren,°   *lost*
> Allas! ȝe while¹ ȝat i was boren.
>
> To sorwe and pine i bringe at eende
> 4   Man ȝat me louet, i schal him schende.°   *harm*
>
> To ȝe fend i owe fewte,°   *fealty*
> Truage,° homage, and gret lewte.   *tribute*

Since the medieval couplet, like the quatrain, ties words and lines together for rhetorical emphasis and not for epigrammatic wit, the rhyme does not surprise, much less dazzle us; it has about it a humble air of rightness. One of the more crisp couplets, for instance, describes what Tutivillus, "þe deuyl of hell," will do to women who chatter during church services:

> But° þai be stil, he wil ham quell,°   *unless; kill*
> Wiþ kene crokes° draw hem to hell,   *hooks*
>   ad puteum autem flentes.   *wailing (as they go) to the pit*
>   (15th:179)

We feel that this is only reasonable, given popular medieval religion; the close syntactic relationships, and the rhyme on quell/hell, all fit together. But the couplet does not "snap" like Pope's inscription for a royal dog collar:

> I am his Highness' Dog at *Kew*;
> Pray tell me Sir, whose Dog are you?[8]

The rhymed couplets in "Tutivillus" have no more epigrammatic brilliance than any two rhyming lines, though they do exist as couplets. Like the rhymes in, say, "O man vnkynde" (p. 96), these have the

¹ the time (þ is represented throughout by ȝ)

same function as other figures of sound: they stress the denotative sense of the words.

The prevailing syntactic rhythm is likewise conducive to a ready grasp of the sense; the structure of the sentences, largely paratactic, lends itself to end-stopped lines and quick aural comprehension. Periodic sentences can be very effective, but they are not common. They are often used to express a cause-and-effect relationship, in which the sense remains suspended until the last few lines, as in this stanza (for the full text, see p. 29):

	So depe ye be	
8	Grauene, parde,°	*by God, indeed*
	With-yn myn hert,	
	That A-fore me	
	Euer I yow see,	
	In thought couert.	

(The parenthetic "parde" in line 8 is a typical and good device for achieving rhythmic variety and a colloquial sense of immediacy.) The closing of the sense is delayed until "see," which receives further emphasis as a rhyme-word; and the last line is an excellent denouement, a much finer stroke of art than it would have been to close with "Euer I yow see." The same kind of hypotaxis occurs in "Quanne hic se on rode":

	Quanne hic se on rode	*When I see on the cross*
	ihesu mi lemman,°	*beloved*
	An be-siden him stonden	
4	marie an Iohan,	
	And his rig° i-suongen,°	*back; flogged*
	and his side i-stungen,	
	for þe luue of man,	
8	Wel ou° hic to wepen	*ought*
	and sinnes for-leten,°	*abandon*
	yif hic of luue kan,	*if I know anything of love*
	yif hic of luue kan,	
12	yif hic of luue kan.	

Here the sense is left open until line 8, which consequently strikes us with great force, a force that sustains itself through the threefold repetition of the last line. Even when the qualifications and parentheses are compounded, as in the second stanza of "This present book"

(p. 23), the relationships are usually clear because logical. And if they are not precisely syllogistic, the connections are nonetheless obvious:

> Go hert, hurt with aduersite,
> And let my lady þi wondis see;
> And sey hir þis, as y say þe:
> 4   far-wel my Ioy, and wel-com peyne,
> til y se my lady Agayne.

(The "reciprocity" in line 3 is another recurrent feature of medieval poems; see, for example, "Tappster, fille Another Ale" (p. 93, ll. 6–8).

But however simple and logical periodic sentences may be, they are by definition less simple than parataxis, which is the main form of syntactic rhythm in these poems. Again, it is helpful to remember that words, the smallest units of syntax, are often bound in symmetrical pairs: "be-þing & se," "Nith & day," "Hand & fotes," "Ded & biriʒed" (14th:70). Similarly, larger units of syntax—phrases, clauses, sentences —also occur in pairs or longer series, as below (for full text, see p. 104):

> Bryng vs in no browne bred, fore þat is mad of brane;
> Nor bryng vs in no whyt bred, fore þer-in is no game,
> But bryng vs in good ale.

Anaphora is a very common rhetorical device, and parallel constructions of all kinds are abundant. The grim mortality poem "Wanne mine eyhnen misten" is a lavish display of anaphora, among other things:

> Wanne mine eyhnen misten,   *when my eyes grow misty*
> and mine heren° sissen,°   *ears; are stopped, cease*
> and mi nose koldet,
> 4 and mi tunge ffoldet,
> and mi rude° slaket,°   *face; slackens*
> And mine lippes blaken,
> and mi muþ grennet,
> 8 and mi spotel° rennet,   *spittle*
> and min her riset,°   *falls*
> and min herte griset,°   *trembles*
> and mine honden biuien,°   *shake*
> 12 and mine ffet stiuien,°   *stiffen*
> al to late, al to late,
> wanne þe bere° ys ate gate.   *bier*
>
> þanne y schel fflutte°   *be carried*
> 16 ffrom bedde te fflore,

	ffrom fflore to here,°	(hair-cloth) shroud
	ffrom here to bere,	
	ffrom bere to putte,°	pit
20	and te putt ffor-dut.°	closed up
	þanne lyd min hus vppe min nose,[1]	
	off al þis world ne gyffe ihic a pese.°	pea

One construction is repeated twelve times and another four times, both within an essentially periodic frame ("when . . . then . . ."). The cumulative effect of so many precisely parallel clauses is plain and emphatic indeed.

Repetition is not used merely for emphasis, however. It can also give rhythmic shape to a poem, as in this crescendo in lines 5 through 7:

	Steddefast crosse, inmong alle oþer	
	þow art a tre mykel° of prise,	great
	in braw(n)che and flore swyl(k) a-noþer°	(object of wot)
4	I ne wot non in wode no rys.[1]	
	swete be þe nalys,	
	and swete be þe tre,	
	and sweter be þe birdyn þat hangis vppon the!	

And the parallels in structure between the first and third lines of the following song provide a counterpoint to the rhyme scheme, allowing the second and fourth lines to function better as asides:

	Her I was and her I drank;	
	far-wyll dam, and mykyll° thank.	much, many
	her I was and had gud cher,	
	and her I drank wyll gud ber.	

Finally, parallelism—in this case, anaphora—can supply the tightly binding force needed in a good couplet, making strict rhyme unnecessary:

> Wit þis ring i wedde þe
> & wit mi bodi i worssepe þe.

Middle English verse has very few of the more complex rhetorical figures, such as the zeugma and chiasmus one associates with Pope. Medieval poets had more use for simple repetition, and they preferred

---

[1] *Then my house lies upon my nose*
[1] *I know of none, in forest or thicket*

to join the members of their sentences in a loose, coordinated manner rather than through subordinate relationships, in order to provide their writing with local structures simple, binding, and emphatic enough to support primary meanings.

6. Large Structures

o far I have discussed only local structures within the poem, devices of sound and rhythm that connect words, phrases, and lines; but there are also structures that give shape and strength to the whole poem. The most important of these larger principles of order are repetition, logic, and such external forms as scriptural narrative, allegory, and miscellaneous formulas like the Ten Commandments or the agricultural calendar. These structures are distinct, in practice, from the smaller devices of sound and rhythm, although certain very general principles, like repetition, may govern local as well as overall organization. All of these procedures are so simple and obvious that we could not hope to find specific sources for them; the medieval *artes poeticae* have, in any case, little to say about general structure (*dispositio*). A good many poets must have drawn principles of organization from sermons, which used such techniques as narrative, logic, balance, and incremental repetition; but this merely tells us that medieval poets were familiar with the art of preaching, as we already know.

Repetition

Repetition of large structural elements is the simplest and one of the most medieval ways of organizing a poem. Although the general meaning of repetition is self-evident, its exact definition involves a few theoretical problems. What constitutes identity? At one end of the scale is verbatim repetition, which we find only in the most primitive songs and nursery rhymes, and in very few of those; at the other end is the broadest kind of resemblance, such as relevance to the same general subject or use of the same level of diction, which hardly qualifies as identity in any usable sense of the term. Between these two limits there is a continuum of possibilities that stress either the constant or the variable element. I shall propose no complete theoretical definition. For the purposes of this study, repetitive structure is the repetition of patterns, in theme or syntax or both, in such a way that the argument

103

or plot does not advance in a straight line, though it may advance circuitously. Repetition need not be verbatim, but it must be the main principle of order in the poem.

I have already discussed small-scale repetition as a means of organization and emphasis. As a principle governing the structure of whole poems, repetition has roughly the same purposes: to stress the basic sense of the verse as heavily as possible, and to provide a very clear form of continuity from one structural unit to the next, by including high proportions of sameness (the constant) to novelty (the variable).

Often, too, repetition is inherent in the very theme or intention of a poem; at a drinking bout, one drinks glass after glass. Thus in "Bryng vs in no browne bred," the syntax itself is almost exactly repeated through eight three-line stanzas, each followed by a two-line burden which in turn repeats the gist of the stanza:

> Bryng vs in good ale, & bryng vs in good ale;
> ffore owr blyssyd lady sak, bryng vs in good ale!
> Bryng vs in no browne bred, fore þat is mad of brane: *made of bran*
> Nor bryng vs in no whyt bred, fore þer-in is no game,° *pleasure*
> But bryng vs in good ale.
>
> 4 Bryng vs in no befe, for þer is many bonys;
> but bryng vs in good ale, for þat goth downe at onys,
>   & bryng vs in good ale.
>
> Bryng vs in no bacon, for þat is passyng fate;
> 8 but bryng vs in god ale, & gyfe vs I-nought of þat,
>   & bryng vs in good ale.
>
> bryng vs in no mutton, for þat is ofte lene;
> Nor bryng vs in no trypys, for þei be syldom clene,
> 12   but bryng vs in good ale.
>
> Bryng vs in no eggys, for þer ar many schelles;
> But bryng vs in good ale, & gyfe vs noþing ellys,
>   & bryng vs in good ale.
>
> 16 Bryng vs in no butter, for þer-in ar many herys;
> Nor bryng vs in no pygges flesh, for þat wyl mak vs borys,° *boars*
>   but bryng vs in good ale.
>
> Bryng vs in no podynges, for þer-in is al gotes° blod; *goat's*
> 20 Nor bryng vs in no veneson, for þat is not for owr good,
>   but bryng vs in good ale.

Bryng vs in no capons flesh, for þat is ofte der;°   *expensive*
Nor bryng vs in no dokes° flesch, for þei slober in þe mer,°   *duck's; pond*
24   but bryng vs in good ale.

The repeated elements are very obvious. There is clearly no progression from the first stanzas to the last, for this type of poem has no beginning or end—only an extended middle. It is profoundly anti-Aristotelian. But even though each stanza has exactly the same import—"bring us in good ale"—phrased in almost exactly the same way, the song contains some surprising turns: we are curious about how the speaker will dismiss the next item in favor of ale. The eight stanzas dispose of brown bread, beef, bacon, mutton, tripe, eggs, butter, pig's flesh, puddings, venison, capon, and duck. The entire interest is in the variation. It is nonetheless a limited interest, which must be reinforced, as in this poem, by strong rhythm and preferably also by music and a festive mood.

Popular songs in general are built on repetition—usually incremental repetition, after the manner of ballads. The notorious "May no man slepe in ȝoure halle" proceeds, with inscrutable logic, from dogs to rats to flies:

           Cantelena   *song*
May no man slepe in ȝoure halle,
for dogges, madame—for dogges, madame;
but ȝyf he haue a tent° of xv ynche   *probe*
4   with twey clogges,°   *wooden blocks (i.e. testicles)*
[to dryve awey the dogges,] madame.
    I-blessyd be such Clogges,
    that ȝyuef such bogges,°   *movements (?)*
8   by-twyne my lady legges,
[to dryve awey the dogges, madame.]

May no man slepe in ȝoure halle,
for rattys, madame—for rattys, madame;
12 but ȝyf he haue a tent of xv enche
    wyt letheryn knappes,°   *knobs*
to dryve awey the rattys, madame.
    I-blessyd be suche knappes,
16   that ȝyveth such swappes,
    vnder my lady lappes,°   *labia*
to dryve awey the rattys, madame.

105

Ma no man slepe in ȝoure [halle,]
20 for flyes, madame—[for flyes, madame;]
but [ȝyf he haue a tent of xv enche]
  [wyt . . . byes°]   *(two) rings*
[to dryve awey the flyes, madame.]
24   I-blessyd be such byes,
    that maketh such suyes,°   *sways, movements*
    by-tuynne my lady thyes,
to dryve awey the flyes, madame.

But the "tent of xv ynche" remains constant, as do the syntax and
rhythm. And the bawdy popular riddle "We bern abowtyn non cattes
skynnys" adds a little more information in each stanza, with the formula "I haue . . . [a pocket, a jelly, a powder]":

We ben chapmen° lyȝt of fote,   *pedlars*
þe fowle weyis° for to fle.   *paths*
We bern abowtyn non cattes skynnys,
pursis, perlis, syluer pynnis,
smale wympeles for ladyis chynnys;
4   damsele, bey sum ware of me.

I haue a poket for þe nonys,
þerine ben tweyne precyous stonys;
damsele, hadde ȝe asayid hem onys,
8   ȝe xuld þe raþere gon with me.

I haue a Ielyf of godes sonde,   *a jelly sent from God*
Withoutyn fyt it can stonde;
It can smytyn & haȝt non honde;   *has no hands*
12   Ryd° ȝourself quat it may be.   *guess*

I haue a powder for to selle,
Quat it is can I not telle—
It makit maydenys wombys to swelle;
16   þerof I haue a quantyte.

But there exist poems of far more complex interest which are
organized by repetition. They belong to the vanity tradition, which,
like the drinking songs, is inherently repetitive; the essential message
is that all of us, one after another, must die, and therefore should repent. Death repeats itself almost infinitely. Critics have rightly praised
such poems as Nashe's "In Time of Plague" and Dunbar's "Lament for
the Makeris,"[1] both more complex than similar poems in Middle Eng-

lish. Both repeat a liturgical refrain after each stanza ("Lord, have mercy on us" and "Timor mortis conturbat me"), and I believe both derive their great power mainly from the perfect congruence of method and theme. The same can be said of a less massive but equally striking poem from the fifteenth century, "I wende to dede," whose quietly terrifying speeches might have been spoken offstage during a performance of the *danse macabre,* while the figures went through the grim pantomime so often painted and engraved during the late Middle Ages:

> I wende to dede, knight stithe° in stoure,°   *strong; battle*
> thurghe fyght in felde i wane þe flour;
> Na fightis me taght þe dede to quell—[1]
> 4 weend to dede, soth i ʒow tell.
>
> I weende [to dede], a kynge I-wisse;
> What helpis honor or werldis blysse?
> Dede is to mane þe kynde° wai—   *natural*
> 8 i wende to be clade in clay.
>
> I wende to dede, clerk ful of skill,
> þat couth with worde men mare & dill.°   *benumb*
> Sone has me made þe dede ane ende—
> 12 beese ware with me! to dede i wende.

The dramatic and graphic qualities of the poem—its setting, its sharp outlines and spare detail—no doubt contribute much to its very moving effect, but I wish here to single out the repetitive structure, which I think is most essential. All three stanzas correspond line for line. In each stanza, the first line begins with "I wende to dede," followed by an appositive phrase briefly defining the speaker; the second line summarizes the speaker's worldly accomplishments; the third states that he is about to die, suggesting an ironic contrast with the preceding line; and the last line returns to the present moment, the actual journey to death. In the last line of the poem, it is appropriate that a *clerk* turns to address the audience, like the "doctor" (a learned clerk) in the morality play. The three stanzas cover three very important social classes; in its complete, exhaustive form, this poem, like the "Lament for the Makeris," would have listed all the estates and perhaps a few extra occupations. Even as it is, "I wende to dede" captures the relentlessness and universality of death, in nearly regular tetrameter couplets

---

[1] *no fights taught me (how) to kill death*

and end-stopped lines, which, combined with the strongly repetitive structure, suggest a somber processional rhythm.

Repetition, then, contributes to a sense of inevitability and truth. It can also deepen an atmosphere of rare mystery, as it does in the famous "Corpus Christi Carol":

> Lully, lulley; lully, lulley;
> The fawcon hath born my mak° away   *mate*
>
> 1
> He bare hym vp, he bare hym down;
> He bare hym into an orchard brown.°   *dark*
>
> 2
> In that orchard ther was an hall,
> That was hangid with purpill and pall.°   *rich draping*
>
> 3
> And in that hall ther was a bede;
> Hit was hangid with gold so rede.
>
> 4
> And yn that bed ther lythe a knyght,
> His wowndes bledyng day and nyght.
>
> 5
> By that bedes side ther kneleth a may,°   *maiden*
> And she wepeth both nyght and day.
>
> 6
> And by that beddes side ther stondith a ston,
> "Corpus Christi" wretyn theron.   *"the Body of Christ"*

Like "We bern abowtyn non cattes skynnys," the carol uses a formula, this time spacial: "In that ... [orchard, hall, bed]." As in certain nursery rhymes, we penetrate closer and closer to the center, the heart of the mystery, which is reserved for the last stanza. Progression is indeed more important here than repetition, although it is the tentative yet deliberate quality of the repeated formula—along with the choice diction, of course—that creates the aura of hieratic mystery.

"He bare hym vp," like all carols and many other poems, has a burden or refrain, a repeated element that can give structural cohesion even to long poems. But the usual repeated element is a theme or syntactic formula that easily reaches the listener and, as in "Old Mother Hubbard" or the still-popular riddle "I have a ȝong suster," draws his attention forward through one variation after another:

108

I haue a ȝong suster
   ffer be-ȝondyn þe se,
many be þe drowryis°   *love-tokens*
4   þat che sente me.

che sente me þe cherye
   with-outyn ony ston,
& so che ded þe dowe°   *dove*
8   with-outyn ony bon.

sche sente me þe brer°   *briar*
   with-outyn ony rynde,°   *branch*
sche bad me loue my lemman
12   with-oute longgyng.

how xuld ony cherye
   be with-oute ston?
& how xuld only dowe
16   ben with-oute bon?

how xuld ony brer
   ben with-oute rynde?
how xuld y loue myn lemman
20   with-out longyng?

Quan þe cherye was a flour,
   þan hadde it non ston.
quan þe dowe was an ey,°   *egg*
24   þan hadde it non bon.

Quan þe brer was on-bred,°   *unborn*
   þan hadde it non rynd.
quan þe maydyn haȝt° þat che louit,   *has*
28   che is with-out longing.

Logic

Next to repetition, the most clear and obvious way to organize a poem is through some simplified form of logic. Many of the short poems are, in fact, essentially syllogisms, explicit or implicit; or at least they include large pieces of straightforward reasoning from axioms to conclusions. This method has distinct advantages for a writer who wishes to persuade his audience, or define a concept, or even to help people enjoy their drinking and eating. Logic is compelling, even to large groups of listeners, if the outline of the argument is plain enough. It is certainly the natural instrument for persuasion and definition, useful to both rhetoricians and philosophers.

In the poems, syllogistic reasoning usually takes the form of a proposition followed by corollaries and conclusions:

> Make we mery bothe more & lasse, *both high and low (socially)*
> ffor now ys þe tyme of crystymas.

> Lett no man cum into this hall—
> Grome, page, nor yet marshall,
> But þat sum sport he bryng with-all,
> 4 for now ys the tyme of crystmas.

> Yff that he say he can not syng,
> sum oder sport then lett hym bryng,
> þat yt may please at thys festyng,
> 8 for now ys the tyme of Crystmas.

> Yff he say he can nowght do,
> Then for my loue aske hym no mo;
> But to the stokkes then lett hym go,
> 12 for now ys þe tyme of crystmas.

Thus nearly each line of this Christmas song begins with or includes a word indicating a logical transition: But that . . . , for . . . , Yff . . . , then . . . , [so] that . . . , for . . . , Yff . . . , then . . . , But . . . , for. . . . Similarly, a well written love poem from the Findern Anthology is organized logically:

> What so men seyn
> loue is no peyn
> to them, serteyn,
> 4 but varians.° *without variation*
> for they constreyn
> ther hertis to feyn,
> ther mowthis to pleyn° *complain*
> 8 ther displesauns.° *displeasure, discontent*
>
> whych is in dede
> butt feynyd drede°— *worry, anxiety*
> so god me spede— *so help me God*
> 12 and dowbilnys:° *hypocrisy*
> ther othis to bede,° *offer*
> ther lyuys to lede;

	and proferith mede°	*reward (object)*
16	new fangellnys.°	*fickleness*

	for when they pray,
	ye shall haue nay;
	what so they sey
20	beware ffor shame.
	ffor euery daye

	they waite ther pray°	*they wait for their prey*
	wher-so they may,	
24	and make butt game.	

	Then semyth me	
	ye may well se	
	they be so fre	
28	in euyry plase,	
	hitt were pete°	*pity*
	butt they shold be	
	be-gelid,° parde,	*beguiled*
32	with-owtyn grase.°	*grace*

It begins with a general statement (ll. 1–4), followed by an explanation (ll. 5–8), amplification (ll. 9–16), further explanations (ll. 17–24), and a crisp conclusion (ll. 25–32). Also, most of the striking effect of "Adam lay I-bowndyn" follows from the oddly strict, deliberate form and substance of its argument: "If . . . not, then . . . not, therefore . . .":

	Adam lay I-bowndyn, bowndyn in a bond,	
	forwe þowsand wynter þowt he not to long;	
	And al was for an appil, an appil þat he tok,	
4	As clerkis fyndyn wretyn in here book.	

	Ne hadde þe appil take ben, þe appil taken ben,	
	ne hadde neuer our lady a ben heuene qwen;	*have been heaven's queen*
	Blyssid be þe tyme þat appil take was,	
8	Þer-fore we mown° syngyn, "deo gracias!"°	*may; "thanks be to God!"*

And the fifteenth-century poem of fortune "There schapeth nought from her intent" supports the general proposition of the first line with explanations (ll. 2, 6), examples (ll. 3–4), and conclusions (ll. 5, 7–8):

When fortune list° yewe° here assent,	*wishes; to give*
What is too deme° þat may be doo?°	*judge; done*

There schapeth° nought from her entent,   *escapes*
ffor as sche will it goth ther-to;
All passith by her iugement,
4   The hy astate, the pore all-so.
    When ffortune.

To lyve in joy out of turment,
Seyng the worlde goth too and fro—
Thus is my schort aviseament,
8   As hyt comyth so lete it go!
    When ffortune.

All of these poems, so different in purpose, have roughly the same logical structure that the schoolmen had been cultivating since the rediscovery of Aristotle.

Not all logical structure, however, is perfectly straightforward and practical; medieval poets could be playful with their logic as well as their liturgy and other serious matters.[2] One of the more light-hearted satires, "I am sory for her sake," makes use of the "self-evident proposition" found in many nursery rhymes:

Care away, away, away,
Murnyng away.
  y am forsake,
  an-oþer ys take,
no more murne yc may.

I am sory for her sake,
  yc may wel ete & drynke;
wanne yc sclepe yc may not wake,
4   so muche on here yc þenke.

I am brout° in suche a bale,   *brought*
  & brout in suche a pyne,
Wanne yc ryse vp of my bed
8   me liste° wel to dyne.   *(I) want*

I am brout in suche a pyne,
  y-brout in suche a bale,
wanne yc haue rythe god wyne   *right good wine*
12   me liste drynke non ale.

The technique is reminiscent of "The Brave Old Duke of York," who marches his men up to the top of a hill, then down again:

And when they were up, they were up,
    And when they were down, they were down,
    And when they were only half-way-up,
      They were neither up nor down.[3]

Slightly less playful, perhaps, is the gnomic epigram "Pees [peace] maketh plente," which proves its thesis by circuitous if not circular logic, moving from "pees" back to "pees" through commenting sharply on the way of the world:

Pees maketh plente.
Plente maketh pryde.
Pryde maketh plee.°   *plea, lawsuit*
4 Plee maketh pouert.°   *poverty*
Pouert makethe pees.

    Much more important than occasional flourishes performed with the logical method is its often binary nature. I have mentioned the blocklike, "rectangular" character of the poems with regard to syntax and versification; the same principle applies to overall structure, because of a certain dualism at the center of many poems. This is to say, once again, that purpose or intention determines structure; an inherent split in the meaning naturally appears in the whole poem, form as well as content. The poets are concerned, for example, with such two-part matter as apparent beauty versus hidden corruption and ugliness, a lovely but cruel lady, or an omnipotent but weak and suffering God. As I have already argued, paradox is of great importance to the Middle English poems; but paradox is not the only reason for their twofold structure. The very prominent pairs of connectives often make logical or temporal contrasts, which are not necessarily paradoxical: then/now, now/soon, since/therefore, if/then.

    The great virtue of these contrasting members is their binding force, which is a virtue of all sound logic. Many of the epigrams, especially, are built on a simple pair of logical terms:

If man him biðocte   *If man bethought himself*
inderlike° & ofte   *inwardly*
hu arde° is te fore°   *hard; go*
4 fro bedde te flore,
hu reuful is te flitte
fro flore te pitte,
fro pitte te pine

113

8   ðat neure sal fine,°   *finish*
    i wene° non sinne   *think*
    sulde his herte winnen.

In these lines, the formula "if *X*, then *Y*" points our expectation, from the very outset, towards the conclusion. We can even anticipate with certainty the form of the conclusion: it must be an implication of *X*, and as we gradually find out what *X* represents, our anticipation of the climax becomes more precise and more eager. The bond between the two poles of the epigram has the magnetic strength of logic; the final lines fall into place with absolute certainty.

Of course this particular epigram also makes skillful use of repetition. The poet has built into his work a tight sequence which has its foundation in the logic of experience and doctrine: the sinner's progress from bed to floor to grave to hellfire. By experience we know that all of us pass from bed to floor to grave; from doctrine and sermons we learn that hardened sinners proceed from grave to hellfire. The whole sequence is actually a narrative, but it is so stereotyped and was so obviously true to a medieval audience that it must have been more convincing than a valid syllogism.

Many other short poems bracket their contents with similar pairs; one such is "Ihesus woundes so wide," which uses if/then:

    Ihesus woundes so wide
    ben welles of lif to þe goode,
    Namely° þe stronde° of hys syde,   *especially; stream*
4 þat ran ful breme° on þe rode.°   *fiercely; rood, cross*

    ʒif þee liste to drinke,   *if you want to drink*
    to fle fro þe fendes of helle,
    Bowe þu doun to þe brinke
8 & mekely taste of þe welle.

Others repeat the balanced relationship with slightly different contents each time, as does "Giff sanct Paullis day" (if/then):

    Giff sanct Paullis day° be fair and cleir,   *June 29*
    Than sal be-tyd ane happie yeir.
    Gif it chances to snaw or rane,
4 Than sal be deir° all kynde of grayne.   *dear, expensive*
    and giff þe wind be hie on loft,
    Than weir° sall vex þe kingdome oft.   *war*
    and gif þe cloudis mak darke þe skye,
8 Boith nowte° and foull that yeir sall dye.   *cattle*

When there is a temporal contrast, it usually juxtaposes a happy or at least acceptable past with an afflicted present, as in this grim variation on "Little Boy Blue":

Wel, qwa° sal thir hornes blau,	*who*
Haly Rod thi day?	*(Holy Cross Day, September 14)*
Nou is he dede and lies law	
Was wont to blaw thaim ay.	*who always used to blow them*

But this is not always the case. One of the most unusual of all the Christmas carols, "Owt of your slepe aryse and wake," proclaims that "*Now* man is brighter than the sonne" (my italics) because Christ is born; formerly man was "thralle" and "smalle":

> Nowel, nowel, nowel,
> Nowel, nowel, nowel!

1

Owt of your slepe aryse and wake,
For God mankynd° nowe hath ytake   *(object)*
Al of a maide without eny make;°   *mate, peer*
  Of al women she bereth the belle.
    Nowel!

2

And thorwe a maide faire and wys
Now man is made of ful grete pris;
Now angelys knelen to mannys seruys,
  And at this tyme al this byfel.
    [Nowel!]

3

Now man is brighter than the sonne;
Now man in heuen an hye shal wone;°   *dwell*
Blessyd be God this game is begonne,
  And his moder emperesse of helle.
    [Nowel!]

4

That euer was thralle, now ys he fre;
That euer was smalle, now grete is she;
Now shal God deme° bothe the and me   *judge*
  Vnto his blysse yf we do wel.
    Nowel!

115

5

Now man may to heuen wende;
Now heuen and erthe to hym they bende;
He that was foo now is oure frende;
   This is no nay that Y yowe telle.
     Nowel!

6

Now, blessyd brother, graunte vs grace
A° domesday to se thy face   *at*
And in thy courte to haue a place,
   That we mow° there synge nowel.   *may*
     Nowel!

And the problematic carol "If thou serue a lord of pryse" (C:381) uses
the stock contrast between the favors and malice of fortune ("Now
thou art gret; tomorwe xal I") to plead for the superiority of the next
world over this one. Medieval poets, more than moderns, were fond of
cleaving their reality in two.

    Naturally, a binary structure is also implicit in any dialogue, just
as repetition is implicit in the use of a burden or refrain. There are
occasional poems which seem, in addition, to reflect the question-and-
answer method of the schools, the *sic et non* of Peter Abelard. The
thirteenth-century "Sey, wist y þe brom" (p. 37) is just such a dialogue.
The housewife puts the question, and the "wist y þe brom" not only
gives an answer, he gives it in the binary "if/then" form.

    Finally, twofold structure can be found even in the absence of
formal, explicit logic. In the two short songs "Mirie it is while sumer
ilast" and "Foweles in þe frith," the basic structure is an implied contrast:

A. [M]irie it is while sumer ilast
    wið fugheles° song,   *bird's*
    oc nu necheð windes blast   *but now the wind's blast draws near*
4 and w[e]der strong.
    Ej! ej! what þis nicht [is] long,
    and ich wid wel michel° wrong   *much*
    soregh° and murne and [fast].   *sorrow*

B. Foweles in þe frith,°   *wood*
    þe fisses in þe flod,
    And i mon waxe wod.   *And I might grow mad*
4 Mulch sorw I walke with
    for beste° of bon and blod.   *the best one*

The first song contrasts good weather with bad, and strongly implies a parallel between the bad weather and the speaker's mood. "Foweles in þe frith" contrasts the birds and fish, who are in their proper places, with the speaker, who is at odds with his world and himself. (Both songs are equally obscure about motives for the speaker's despondency; this is perhaps a built-in weakness of the indirect method.) But whether or not binary structure appears in a strict logical form, it lends itself very well to the needs of Middle English poets, who often wished to clamp the major parts of their compositions together.

As a consequence of two-part structure and, more generally, of the logical method, the last line of a medieval poem is often extremely powerful and important. It may state the only alternative to a good or disastrous course of action, or perhaps it may define such truths as make the difference between eternal life and eternal death. For any number of specific reasons, the final line can be truly final: definitive, inescapable, and immensely resonant.

Most of the poems with strong endings are epigrams, which tightly compress their strength; they are like springs to be released with a final touch—the last line. "Louerd, þu clepedest me" closes with an understatement that suggests, very subtly, the enormity of delaying one's response to a divine summons:

Louerd, þu clepedest° me	*called*
an ich nagt° ne ansuarede þe	*naught*
Bute wordes scloe and sclepie:	*slow and sleepy*
4 "þole° yet! þole a litel!"	*endure, wait*
Bute "yiet" and "yiet" was endelis,	
and "þole a litel" a long wey is.	

In a similar vein, and making similar use of comprehensive words, is "Euen [heaven], it es a richȝ ture" (p. 84). After briefly describing the joys of heaven, the poet reminds "Sinful man" that unless he abandons sin, he will be eternally singing "wailaway," "for comes þu neuer mare þar-I[nne]." And the insouciant epitaph for "Riche Alane" has the most brilliantly pointed conclusion of all the poems, enhanced, it is true, by the rhyme:

Here lyeth vnder þis marbyll ston,	
Riche Alane, þe ballid° man;	*bald*
Wheþer he be safe or noght,	
I recke° neuer—for he ne roght!	*care; for he didn't care*

But surely the most deeply moving last line is the one in which Christ, after the Crucifixion, looks forward to his Second Coming (for the full text, see p. 36):

> and thane schall know both devyll and mane,
> What I was and what I ame.

All of these strong endings are, along with binary structure, a natural by-product of the logical method, which, like the repetition of similar themes or formulas, lends an appropriate kind of order to the anonymous short poem: it compels one's intellect and emotions, and it provides a firm, highly intelligible frame for the poem's meaning—a frame that could accommodate many specific meanings and serve many different purposes.

External Forms

Repetition and logic are highly abstract methods for generating the sequence of elements in a poem; they are rules of procedure true only to themselves, like the hidden key to certain items on intelligence tests (if you notice that the rule is to multiply by two and subtract three, you can predict the rest of the numerical series). But external forms are given from the outside, from areas of thought and experience not directly related to literary methods. In the Middle English lyrics, the most important external forms are allegories, "icons," narratives, and various kinds of formulas. All of these are distinctively medieval in that they are usually based on Christian culture, and are therefore accessible to a wide public. Stephen Manning's definition of "religious forms" is quite relevant here, though the forms I am concerned with are not necessarily religious: "By religious forms . . . I mean a generally accepted formulation of any phase of the spiritual life which automatically enables the poet to arrange his materials in some kind of sequence."[4]

The most obvious example of familiar narrative is the Christmas story, which, like other narratives based on Scripture, especially the Passion and Easter sequence, provides a universally clear structure for a great many songs and poems. A macaronic carol like "Jhesus, almyghty Kyng of Blys" (C:23B) can describe and interpret the Annunciation, Nativity, and visit of the Magi half in Latin and still run no serious risk of losing its audience. Even the more idiosyncratic narratives are quite open and public by modern standards:

Mery hyt ys in may mornyng
Mery wayys ffor to gonne.

And By a chapell as y Came,
Mett y wyhte Ihū to chyrcheward gone[1]
Petur and Pawle, thomas & Ihon,
4 And hys desyplys Euēry-chone.
    Mery hytt ys.

Sente Thomas þe Bellys gane° ryng,   *(indicates past tense: "did ring")*
And sent Collas° þe mas gane syng,   *St. Nicholas*
sente Ihoñ toke þat swete offeryng,
8 And By a chapell as y Came.
    Mery hyt ys.

Owre lorde offeryd whate he wollde,
A challes alle off ryche rede gollde;
Owre lady, þe crowne off hyr mowlde,° *head*
12 The sone owte off hyr Bosome schone.
    Mery hyt ys.

Sent Iorge þat ys owre lady knyȝte,
He tende þe tapyrys fayre & Bryte—
To myn yȝe a semley syȝte,
16 And By a chapell as y Came.
    Mery hyt ys.

The speaker of this poem observes some strange and beautiful things by any standard, but all that he sees on his walk is, in a sense, familiar to any medieval Christian: Christ and his apostles, the Virgin Mary, St. Nicholas, St. George, and a celebration of the eucharist complete with bells, candles, and lavish offerings. When a modern poet takes a walk, it is essentially a private affair. Thus John Crowe Ransom, in the course of a poetic stroll, observes what is no doubt a conventional old southern manor; but he nonetheless describes a particular house and gives his particular, private response to it:

> But on retreating I saw myself in the token
> How loving from my foreign weed the feather curled
> On the languid air; and I went with courage shaken
> To dip, alas, into some unseemlier world.[5]

Medieval allegories are only a little less part of the public domain than scriptural narratives,[6] but they compensate for whatever exotic

---

[1] *I met with Jesus going churchward*

flavor they may have by their doggedly systematic schemes, which were defined by tradition and by the authors of popular religious manuals, not by the poets (who may, of course, also happen to have written manuals). A Christmas carol with allegorical structure is "Lyth and lystyn, both old and yyng, / How the rose begane to spryng,"[7] which allegorizes the five joys of Mary as five branches of a rose springing from Mary's bosom:

> Of a rose, a louely rose,
> Of a rose I syng a song.
>
> 1
>
> Lyth° and lystyn, both old and yyng,   *listen*
> How the rose begane to spryng;
> A fayyrer rose to owr lekyng
>   Sprong ther neuer in kynges lond.
>
> 2
>
> v branchis of that rose ther ben,
> The wych ben both feyer and chene;°   *lovely*
> Of a maydyn, Mary, hevyn quene,
>   Ovght° of hyr bo[s]um the branch sprong. *out*
>
> 3
>
> The [first] branch was of gret honour:
> That blyssed Mary shuld ber the flour,
> Ther cam an angell ovght hevyn toure
>   To breke the develes bond.
>
> 4
>
> The secund branch was gret of myght,
> That sprong vpon Cristmes nyght;
> The sterre shone and lemeghd° bryght, *gleamed*
>   That man schul se it both day and nyght.
>
> 5
>
> The third branch gan° spryng and spred; *did*
> iii kynges than to branch gan led
> Tho to owr Lady in hure chyldbed;
>   Into Bethlem that branch sprong ryght.
>
> 6
>
> The fourth branch, it sprong to hell,
> The deueles powr for to fell,
> That no sovle therin shuld dwell,
>   The brannch so blessedfully sprong.

7

The fifth branch, it was so swote,°   *sweet,*
Yt sprong to hevyn, both croppe° and rote, *top*
In euery ball° to ben owr bott,°   *bale; remedy*
 So blessedly yt sprong.

In this as in other allegorical poems, the strict sequence of well known doctrinal elements aids the memory as well as the understanding.

Some poems, allegorical at first sight, are really extended metaphors that serve as "verbal icons":

Man, folwe seintt Bernardes trace° *track, model*
And loke in ihesu cristes face,
How hee lut° hys heued° to þe   *bows; head*
4 Swetlike for to kessen þe,
And sprat° hise armes on þe tre,   *spreads*
Senful men, to klippen° þe.   *embrace*
In sygne of loue ys open his syde;
8 Hiis feet y-nayled wid þe tabyde.° *to abide*
Al his bodi is don on rode,
Senful man, for þyne goode.

These striking lines anticipate the seventeenth-century "poetry of meditation"; we are invited to visualize the scene, for the sake of devotion and repentance. The familiar details of this late medieval Crucifixion are quasi-allegorized, but the whole ensemble does not add up to an allegory. There is no narrative, and the details do not have analogues in a transcendent scheme of values; they incorporate those values themselves. The whole poem is a traditional metaphor, realized by interpreting the face, arms, wounded side, and nailed feet in relation to all of us as we look on: Christ is the Lover of man, for all time. Whenever we think of the Crucifixion or see a crucifix, its details will henceforth unavoidably remind us, very graphically, that Christ is our Lover.

Poems built on formulas also have real mnemonic value. Formulas are often principles of order, in fact, precisely because medieval people wanted to remember them; and the strong rhythm and end-stopped lines of English verse were good for prompting one's memory. "Wanne i ðenke ðinges ðre" uses the common sequence of three, much like some allegorical poems, in order to inculcate in its audience a moral lesson:

121

Wanne i ðenke ðinges ðre
ne mai hi neure bliðe ben:

ðe ton is dat i sal awei,
4 ðe toþer is i ne wot wilk dei.
ðe ðridde is mi moste kare,
I ne wot wider i sal faren.°

the one is that I must (go) away
the other is that I don't know which day

go

Other formulas are based directly on Scripture or tradition, such as
the Ten Commandments (13th:70B), the Paternoster (15th:53), and
the Hail Mary (Cam:11). But religious formulas, like the logical method, can also be used for irreverent purposes; the scurrilous "Joly Jan-
kin" synchronizes a lengthy seduction with the liturgy of the mass
(opening words, epistle, sanctus, agnus dei, and the climactic final
blessing and "Deo gracias"):

"kyrie," so "kyrie,"
Iankyn syngyt merie,
with "aleyson."
As I went on ʒol day in owr prosessyon,
Knew I Ioly Iankyn be his mery ton.
[*kyrieleyson.*][1]

4 Iankyn be-gan þe offys° on þe ʒol day,   *office*
    & ʒyt me þynkyt it dos me good, so merie gan° he say *did*
    kyrieleyson.

Iankyn red þe pystyl ful fayr & ful wel,
8 & ʒyt me þinkyt it dos me good, as euere haue I sel.[2]
    [*kyrieleyson.*]

Iankyn at þe sanctus crakit a merie note,
    & ʒyt me þynkyt it dos me good—I payid for his cote.[3]
12   [*kyrieleyson.*]

Iankyn crakit notes an hunderid on a knot.[4]
    & ʒyt he hakkyt hem smaller þan wortes° to þe pot. *herbs*
    k[*yrieleyson.*]

16 Iankyn at þe angnus beryt þe pax brede,[5]
    he twynkelid,° but sayd nowt, & on myn fot he trede. *winked*
    [*kyrieleyson.*]

[1] *"Lord have mercy," with pun on "Alison"*
[2] *as I ever hope to have bliss (heaven)*
[3] *I paid for his "cutting" (of the notes) (?)*
[4] *a hundred at once*
[5] *"peace-bread," kissed during mass*

Benedicamus domino,[6] cryst fro schame me schylde.
20   Deo gracias þerto[7]—alas, I go with schylde!
     k[*yrieleyson.*]

Finally, to close on a more sober note, even the farmer's calendar could give total structure to a poem (see "By thys fyre I warme my handys," p. 95).

Formulas, allegories, and narratives, together with logic and repetition, are all principles of gross structure which, either by means of clear, convincing sequence, or very widespread currency, or both, were able to organize a good variety of materials for several different purposes, and were thus able to convey these themes and purposes to broad classes of listeners. In this effort the large structural schemes were buttressed by the devices for local organization: binding, emphatic, and simple meters, figures of sound, and relationships among units of verse and syntax.

[6] *Let us bless the Lord*
[7] *Thanks be to god, as well*

7. Conclusion

o far I have juxtaposed the Middle English lyric only with modern poems, for maximum contrast. But there are other, more subtle points of contrast and resemblance, which, like coordinates on a five- or six-dimensional graph, will allow us to locate the Middle English lyric with greater precision. First, there are lyric traditions in other late medieval languages, such as Old French, Middle High German, and Medieval Latin; these are of interest mainly insofar as they differ from their English counterpart. Second, there are native short poems written before and after the Middle English period, from Anglo-Saxon and sixteenth-century England; these are valuable for their resemblances to the Middle English lyric. This array of contrasts and similarities will help define both the local and the more general qualities of the medieval English tradition.

Medieval Contemporaries

I will attempt no overall comparison between the Middle English lyric and the other medieval traditions; the literature in each language is vast, they all differ from each other, and any such comparison, even if possible, would be irrelevant. I am interested in only one significant point of comparison. Throughout this study I have stressed the impersonal, generalized, public quality of the Middle English poems; the poets show practically no interest in subtle, unique experiences and feelings, neither their own nor anyone else's. They are anonymous. But a large number of medieval poets writing in German, French, and Latin do show such interest; they had discovered, or rediscovered, the nuances of personality as a subject for verse, and in most cases their names have been preserved—a fact of symbolic importance. Virtually all the recurrent traits of the Middle English lyric can be found, to varying degrees, in the other three bodies of poetry. But this seemingly modern feature of the lyrics in German, Latin, and French cannot be found among those in English, at least not to any comparable extent.

Contemporary with the very first lyrics in Middle English, the German-speaking Walther von der Vogelweide (c. 1170–c. 1230) had already developed the lyric art of *self*-expression far beyond anything to be achieved in English for three hundred years. His immediate predecessors, the minnesingers Heinrich von Morungen and Reinmar von Hagenau (Walther's master, then his rival) had written courtly love songs, in which the poet's theme, feelings, and style were carefully prescribed by convention; Reinmar, in particular, granted himself no room to express eccentric, personal feelings. But Walther impressed his personality on poem after poem, by suggesting attitudes and by directly taking himself as theme. He swears that he would sooner eat raw crabs or become a monk at Toberlû (known for its austerity) than endure for long the miseries of winter. In a different mood, he proclaims "I've got my fief, all the world, I've got my fief! Now I'm not afraid of February at my toes . . . . I've been poor too long without my consent; I was so full of abusive words that my breath stank . . ."[1] And his great *ubi sunt* poem, "Owê war sint verswunden alliu mîniu jâr" ("Alas, where have all my years vanished to"), is deeply personal in its review and judgment of Walther's own past, present, and wishes for the future.

These poems and many others deal with his own life, but Walther can extend his psychological insight beyond himself. His most celebrated lyric, "Under der linden," is a monologue by a young girl, whose feelings are rendered in minutely controlled strokes of language:

> Under the lime tree
> On the heather,
> Where we had shared a place of rest,
> 4 Still you may find there,
> Lovely together,
> Flowers crushed and grass down-pressed.
> Beside the forest in the vale,
> 8 Tándaradéi,
>   Sweetly sang the nightingale.
>
> I came to meet him
> At the green:
> 12 There was my truelove come before.
> Such was I greeted—
> Heaven's Queen!—
> That I am glad for evermore.

16 Had he kisses? A thousand some:
    Tándaradéi,
        See how red my mouth's become.

    There he had fashioned
20 For luxury
    A bed from every kind of flower.
    It sets to laughing
    Delightedly
24 Whoever comes upon that bower;
    By the roses well one may,
    Tándaradéi,
        Mark the spot my head once lay.

28 If any knew
    He lay with me
    (May God forbid!), for shame I'd die.
    What did he do?
32 May none but he
    Ever be sure of that—and I,
    And one extremely tiny bird,
    Tándaradéi,
36   Who will, I think, not say a word.

    Under der linden
    an der heide,
    dâ unser zweier bette was,
4   *dâ mugt ir vinden*
    schône beide
    gebrochen bluomen unde gras.
    Vor dem walde in einem tal,
8   *tandaradei,*
    schône sanc diu nahtegal.

    Ich kam gegangen
    zuo der ouwe:
12 *dô was mîn friedel komen ê.*
    Dâ wart ich enpfangen
    (hêre frouwe!)
    daz ich bin sælic iemer mê.
16 *Kust er mich? Wol tûsentstunt:*
    tandaradei,
    seht wie rôt mir ist der munt.
    Dô het er gemachet

20   *alsô rîche*
      von bluomen eine bettestat.
      Des wirt noch gelachet
      innerclîche,
24   *kumt iemen an daz selbe pfat:*
      bî den rôsen er wol mac,
      tandaradei,
      merken wâ mir 'z houbet lac.

28   *Daz er bî mir læge,*
      wesse'z iemen
      (nu enwelle got!), sô schamt ich mich.
      Wes er mit mir pflæge,
32   *niemer niemen*
      bevinde daz, wan er und ich,
      und ein kleinez vogellîn:
      tandaradei,
36   *daz mac wol getriuwe sîn.*

The quality of emotion is extremely delicate. The girl is both modest and proud, coy and quietly triumphant. That the experience is fresh in her memory, and that she dwells on it lovingly, is suggested by the continued, lingering existence of the actual bed, which she mentions twice at some length (ll. 4–6, 22–27). The power of the hinting in lines 13 through 15 and 31 through 36 is increased by her parenthetic, strong exclamations (ll. 14, 30), by the affectionate double diminutive in line 34, and by the superb understatement in the last line. I mention only a few of Walther's achievements in this poem, but they are enough to demonstrate a kind and degree of sophistication that medieval English poets almost never attempted.

    Walther's successors were also interested in themselves as poetic subjects, in a more and more coarsely realistic fashion. Neidhart von Reuental (fl. 1230) wrote spring songs about his triumphs among the peasant girls, and winter songs about his failures. Berthold Steinmar (fl. 1280),[2] whose sculptured figure on the Strassburg Cathedral shows him lifting an immense cup to his lips, praises his own throat because it can devour a large goose without choking; and in a love poem he notes that his heart "jumps back and forth like a pig in a sack" ("Als ein swîn in einem sacke / vert mîn herze hin und dar"). Late in the Middle Ages an Austrian nobleman, Oswald von Wolkenstein

(1377–1445), wrote in great technical detail about his travels and forni-
cations. And a man known only as the Monk of Salzburg (late fourteenth century), together with many other poets nameless and named,
celebrates with special gusto the joys of autumn: sausages, wines, roast
pigs and chickens, the Martinmas goose. Even the meanest versifier can
give us a real sense of his own direct physical enjoyment.

The medieval Latin poets also wrote about their own experience,
in verses that tend to be more polished and more satirical than those in
German. Hugh Primas of Orléans (fl. c. 1150) curses the chaplain who
tricked him out of his money and threw him from a cathedral *hospitium*
into the wind and the mud, and he curses a bishop who gave him, in
wintertime, a cloak with no lining. The famous Archpoet, a German
who died around 1165, has fascinated readers for the last eight hundred
years with the intense vitality of his Confession to Rainald von Das-
sel, Archchancellor of the Empire ("Aestuans intrinsecus"—"Inwardly
raging"). And the so-called *Carmina Burana*, a late thirteenth-century
manuscript from the Benediktbeuren monastery in Bavaria, includes
lyrics as complex in tone and attitude as Walther's "Under der linden."
One of these, indeed, is written through a persona much more remote
from the poet than Walther's young lady, yet it contains real subtleties
of feeling; it is the lament of a roast swan:

> The lakes I swam upon,
> My beauty—all is gone.
> 3   I was once a swan.
> >   Alas, alack,
> >   Now I am black,
> >   And burnt both front and back.
>
> Air is my element,
> And water. I resent
> 6   Stifling in condiment.
> >   Alas, alack, etc.
>
> Whiter once than snow,
> The fairest bird I know
> 9   Is blacker than a crow.
> >   Alas, alack, etc.
>
> The scullions watch with glee.
> The flames burn savagely.
> 12   Now they are serving me.
> >   Alas, alack, etc.

Here on a tray I lie,
Unable hence to fly.
15   Gnashing teeth draw nigh.
    Alas, alack,
    Now I am black,
    And burnt both front and back.

Olim lacus colueram,
Olim pulcher extiteram,
3   *Dum cignus ego fueram.*
    Miser, miser,
    Modo niger
    Et ustus fortiter.

Mallem in aquis vivere
Nudo semper sub aere,
6   *Quam in hoc mergi pipere.*
    Miser, miser, etc.

Eram nive candidior,
Quavis ave formosior,
9   *Modo sum corvo nigrior.*
    Miser, miser, etc.

Girat, regirat garcifer;
Me rogus urit fortiter:
12   *Propinat me nunc dapifer.*
    Miser, miser, etc.

Nunc in scutella jaceo,
Et volitare nequeo.
15   *Dentes fredentes video.*
    Miser, miser,
    Modo niger
    Et ustus fortiter.[3]

The lugubrious refrain, the *ubi sunt* suggestions of the first and third stanzas, the comically pitiful, simpleminded statements of the second and last stanzas, combined with the immediacy of lines 11 and 12 and the fine horrendousness of line 15—all of this amounts to a kind of naïvely boastful, pedantic, yet well motivated terror from an absurd point of view. We can afford to enjoy the agonies of a roast swan.

    Medieval French lyrics also display the quirks of private psychology, often in a quite engaging way. The French poets were especially skilled at handling minor themes of very broad interest, like food

129

and weather.[4] Colin Muset, in the middle of the thirteenth century, tells us how much better it is to sit by a fire, with capons turning on the spit and plenty of good wine, than to go out and ravage the countryside as the barons are wont to do; and he sends his song "to Sailly, to Guy who understands reason . . . to see whether or not I'm doing well" ("A Sailli, Guion / Que entent raison / Envoi ma chanson, / Voir se je fais bien ou non"). In the next century, Eustaches Deschamps (1346–1407) composed a good many poems about his own experience, including one delightful rondeau, apparently written after a trip to Bohemia in the service of King Charles VI: "Twenty people eating from two plates, bitter and sour beer to drink, sleeping badly in dark rooms on straw and ordure, lice, fleas, stink, and pigs—this is the essence of Bohemia . . ." ("Vint gens mangier en deux plateaux, / Boire cervoise amere et sure, / Mal couchier, noir, paille et ordure, / Poux, puces, puor et pourceaux / Est de Behaigne la nature . . .").

But the most insistently, savagely personal poet of the Middle Ages was, of course, François Villon (1431–1463 or later). His two great Testaments, full of obscene mockery and deep poignance, contain most of what he wrote; his theme from beginning to end is his own life, and his chosen form—that of a last will and testament—is perfectly suited to his theme. Among the miscellaneous poems, however, there occurs an epigram that briefly and sharply illustrates the poet's cast of mind. It was probably written during one of his many stays in prison:

> I am Françoys, which is no pleasure,
> Born in Paris near Pontoise;
> And soon my neck, by a rope measure,
> Will learn how much my bottom weighs.
>
> *Je suis Françoys, dont il me poise,*
> *Né de Paris emprès Pontoise,*
> *Et de la corde d'une toise*
> *Sçaura mon col que mon cul poise.*[5]

These four lines contain at least three self-deprecating jokes. The "poise" in the first line (it rhymes with "weighs," in Villon's French) suggests weight, a sense amply reinforced in the "poise" of the fourth line; a closer English version might be "I am Françoys, a fact which oppresses (or burdens) me." To speak of being born in Paris near Pontoise is like saying one was "born in London, a place near Slough." The wordplay in the last line, on *col/cul*, is more obvious. The whole epigram is a piece of concentrated self-irony, proceeding from intense awareness of language and of self, in just about equal proportions.

In England and Scotland, the very next generation after Villon was to produce the first lyric poets at all comparable to him, John Skelton (c. 1460–1529) and William Dunbar (c. 1465–c. 1530). An earlier English poet, Thomas Hoccleve (c. 1369–c. 1450), had written about his own daily life, but with little skill. I am sure the different historical situation on the continent had much to do with the early appearance there of marked poetic interest in personality; there were many small courts in Germany and France that patronized the troubadours' art, which, being mainly concerned with love, was inherently psychological. In Germany and Austria, for instance, the development of what we might call poetic individualism could be traced from Walther through Neidhart to men like Oswald von Wolkenstein, all of whom belonged in some sense to the courtly love tradition. And the system of patronage encouraged begging songs, complaints of poverty, and the like, which are often very intimate in tone. There were not as many courts in England as on the continent, and during King Stephen's reign (1135–1154),[6] as Provençal song was first spreading through France, the English barons were at work destroying each other. But I believe the linguistic situation largely determined the more general, practical nature of Middle English verse. It is well known that the prestige of the English language was low, compared to French and Latin; until 1385, schoolboys even construed their Latin in French, not in their native English. Latin was good for erudition, French for elegance, and English for homilies and drinking songs, since most of the common people understood nothing else. Thus religious and popular verse would be written in English, and courtly lyrics would usually not be written at all, at least not until the fifteenth century; the Harley collection is anomalous. But even counting the most personal, immediate lyrics in Middle English, poets with anything like a modern sense of self did not appear in Britain until the eve of the sixteenth century.

English Ancestors and Descendants

I have already mentioned similarities in theme and tone between certain Middle English poems and the Anglo-Saxon elegies, such as

"The Ruin" and "The Wanderer," and I have cited a few lyrics from the Findern Anthology for their tonal and rhythmic resemblance to some of Wyatt's songs (pp. 29 and 110). The most striking and important marks of lyric continuity, from Anglo-Saxon England through the sixteenth century, are neither mainly stylistic/structural nor mainly thematic but both at once, because form and content imply each other. That is, the wish to create Germanically impressive, heroic feelings and language will affect the diction, meter, and rhetoric of Old English poetry as well as its themes, just as Petrarchan modes of erotic feeling will require, in the sixteenth century, a new relationship between syntax and line. But because the analytic framework of this study is essentially formal, I will use formal categories in relating Anglo-Saxon and sixteenth-century lyrics to those of the Middle English period, rather than list thematic parallels, which will in any case be obvious from my discussion. The broad differences among these three periods, which are even more obvious, do not concern us here; and my treatment of the similarities will not be exhaustive.

Besides the elegies, Anglo-Saxon gnomic verse offers especially good points of comparison with the Middle English. The following lines are from the eleventh-century manuscript Cotton Tiberius B I, though the sentiments had probably been handed down from time out of mind:

> The king shall hold the realm. Cities are seen from afar,
> skillful work of giants, those that are on this earth,
> splendid work of wall-stones. Wind is swiftest in air,
> 4   thunder loudest at times. The glories of Christ are great.
>   Fate is strongest. Winter is coldest,
>   spring most frosty—it is cold the longest,
>   summer most bright with sun; the heaven is hottest,
> 8   autumn most glory-blessed; it brings to men
>   the harvest-fruits, those that God sends them.

> *Cyning sceal rice healdan. Ceastra beoð feorran gesyne,*
> *orðanc enta geweorc, þa þe on þysse eorðan syndon,*
> *wrǣtlic weallstana geweorc. Wind byð on lyfte swiftust,*
> 4   *þunar byð þragum hludast. þrymmas syndan Cristes myccle,*
>   *wyrd byð swiðost. Winter byð cealdost,*
>   *lencten hrimigost (he byð lengest ceald),*
>   *sumor sunwlitegost (swegel byð hatost),*
> 8   *hærfest hreðeadegost, hæleðum bringeð*
>   *geres wæstmas, þa þe him god sendeð.*[7]

These verses are what Renaissance critics might call an extreme case of Senecanism: the poem falls into dense, discrete *sententiae*, which are so self-contained that overall structure is barely visible, except for the parts that deal with seasons and weather. It is not fair, in fact, to judge these maxims as a poem in the usual sense. But the fragmented structure of the whole is convenient because it reveals, with particular clarity, the end-stop lines, the parallel syntax, and the proverbial generalizing quality that we find in the Middle English lyric. Each statement is explicit and all-inclusive, like the later proverbs, commonplaces, and moral generalizations. Even in the more descriptive lines (1–3), the nouns, which refer to common realities, are not sharply, sensuously modified; the adjectives in this passage are evaluative or only broadly descriptive (*orðanc, wrætlic*), like the adjectives elsewhere applied to nature (*swiftust, hludast, cealdost*, etc.). And there are no metaphors or other figures of thought. All these features of Anglo-Saxon verse, as well as less developed forms of alliteration, can be found in the Middle English lyric.

Most of them can also be found in the sixteenth-century lyric, in what Wesley Trimpi calls "the native tradition of the plain style."[8] Among the early Renaissance practitioners of this style are Wyatt, Lord Vaux, Barnabe Googe, Gascoigne, Turberville, and Raleigh. Sir Thomas Wyatt (c. 1503–1542), at the beginning of the century, and Sir Walter Raleigh (c. 1552–1618), who lived well into the next century, will serve to illustrate how medieval ways of writing survived the Middle Ages. Here is a lesser-known epigram by Wyatt:

> Patiens, for I have wrong,
>   And dare not shew whereyn,
> Patiens shalbe my song,
> 4   Sins truthe can no thing wynne;
> Patiens then for this fytt,
> Hereafter commis not yett.[9]

The syntax stops at the end of each line, and, though the meter is more regular and finely adjusted to meaning than in medieval lyrics, the major stresses are still heavier and more evenly spaced than, say, in a Shakespeare sonnet. Repetition, parallelism, and logic are the principles of structure: "Patiens" occurs three times in the same position; the three couplets are roughly parallel in syntax; and the general form of the poem is a logical argument in favor of patience, complete with explanations, evidence, conclusions, and the usual syntactic words ("*for*

I have wrong," "*Sins* truthe," "*Patiens then*"). And to fasten down his argument, Wyatt appeals to a proverbial truth (l. 4). The key word, "patience," is very broad abstract noun referring to a moral value, as are "wrong" and "truthe," and there are neither metaphors nor adjectives in the poem. The only hint of the Renaissance here is in the situation itself: Wyatt, speaking to himself like one of Shakespeare's soliloquizers, recommends a stoic virtue.

Raleigh preserves medieval habits of thought and composition long after the new Italian and classical modes have been assimilated. In his short poem "On the Life of Man"[10] ("What is our life? a play of passion"), he methodically extends the metaphor in the first line, like a medieval poet working out the detailed implications of Christ as Lover (p. 121); and in the sonnet to his son ("three things there bee that prosper vp apace") the structure is explicit and numerical. A more obviously "medieval" poem, however, is "The Lie," from which I will quote the first two stanzas and the last:

> Goe soule the bodies guest
>   vpon a thankelesse arrant,
> Feare not to touch the best
> 4   the truth shall be thy warrant:
> Goe since I needs must die,
>   and giue the world the lie.
>
> Say to the Court it glowes,
> 8   and shines like rotten wood,
> Say to the Church it showes
>   whats good, and doth no good.
> If Church and Court reply,
>   then giue them both the lie.
>
> . . . .
>
> So when thou has as I,
>   commanded thee, done blabbing,
> although to giue the lie,
> 76   deserues no lesse then stabbing,
> Stab at thee he that will
>   no stab thy soule can kill.

This poem displays the same rhythmic, syntactic, and metrical traits as the Wyatt epigram. Its structure is also based on logic and repetition, but repetition is by far the more important: the whole poem is a list of extremely various items, one or two per stanza, all of which must be given the lie. This bare repetition, with no attempt to build a crescendo, gives a strong sense that lies and failures are so many and so diverse as to be omnipresent. The logical "if/then" formula, or one of its variants, ties the knot at the end of each stanza but the last, which breaks the pattern for emphasis. The main nouns are again large concepts—moral, social, philosophical—which neither receive nor require much qualification from adjectives, although several of the nouns are set into metaphors: "soule the bodies guest" is a standard figure from the homiletic tradition, but the simile in lines 7 and 8 is not; such close observation of natural process is rare in the medieval lyrics.

These poems of Raleigh and Wyatt, embodying, as they do, so many features of the Middle English tradition, are a fair sample of the sixteenth-century native plain style, which is obviously much closer to the Middle English lyric than the Anglo-Saxon gnomes and elegies are; yet the kinship among the short poems of all three periods is unmistakable, and not at all surprising.

The Middle English Lyric

The anonymous lyrics in Middle English make up a single tradition, public in status and shaped by practical intentions; in nearly all respects, they are distinctively general, impersonal, and anonymous. (Among the few lyric poets who are not anonymous are Thomas Hoccleve, who had little talent; and Dunbar and Skelton, who lived well into the sixteenth century.) The generalness of the poems—their commonplaces and proverbs, their relative lack of modifiers, the self-explaining metaphors, the universally clear and accepted ways of organizing sounds, rhythms, and structures—is responsible for their peculiar excellence; and their excellence is of two kinds. The medieval poets, concerned as they were with purveying general knowledge and attitudes to large classes of people, cultivated, above all, the art of statement; secondarily, they exploited certain resources of diction in the language available to them. Most of the poems I have quoted, which I chose for quality as well as to illustrate specific points, are distinguished in one or both of these respects.

Since many of the poems are essentially statements, their virtues are often the same as the virtues of effective statement: clarity, precision, and concise forcefulness. Thus the best poems are commonly the shortest; they are graphic, definitive epigrams which select the most striking and characteristic traits of their subject. The traits are often extreme, in some sense; and the subject, often of great human significance in itself, provides the real force behind the poem. "I wende to dede" (p. 107), for example, pits maximum human abilities against the power of death, to show the immenseness of that power; and it names the distinctive properties of knight, king, and clerk with precision and brevity. Mortality is in fact the usual heavy weapon of these poets, though religious doctrine can supply as great or even greater force, as in "I haue laborede sore" (p. 36). In any case, the most powerfully moving poems are usually eschatological; they are concerned with the *quattuor hominum novissima*—death, judgment, heaven, and hell.

But cliché is endemic to such poems because their subject matter is, at least in theory, finite and exhaustible, unlike the infinitely nuanced, private, psychological matter of recent poets. The Middle English poets dealt in large blocks of received ideas, defined mostly by doctrine and tradition, and inherently stable. How many ways are there to say that all of us will die and must therefore repent? Or that we must repay Christ by changing our lives, since he suffered and died for us? It may be that the best poems of each kind are those that most compactly fulfill the potential of that kind—realize its entelechy, so to speak. But it is useless to attempt a general description of poetic excellence; a good poet is not quite predictable, and his artistry can show through the smallest details. Perhaps the most that one can say is that the essence of good "anonymous short poems" is shortness, as opposed to verbosity, and a spare, generalized anonymity, as opposed to a detailed subjectivism.

It is certain, however, that as a result of their common "general" nature and intentions, Middle English short poems of various subgenres are stylistically closer to each other than are later versions of the same subgenres. In the Middle Ages, the poetic subjects were all on a roughly similar and high level of abstraction; death, Christ, Mary, sin, the courtly lady, and other major subjects were in essence general phenomena, in spite of the Franciscan efforts to make devotion

more personal. But in the course of a few centuries, the theoretical un-
derpinning of all these broad cultural values, except death, gradually
collapsed or at least changed. In England especially, the cult of the Virgin was all but destroyed by the Reformation; theories of courtly love
also went out of fashion; new doctrines of God, Christ, sin, evil, and
other Christian values arose in Protestant and, later, in largely secular
societies. Instead of praising an ideal of womanhood and telling people
to abandon sin, poets like John Donne wrote about particular women
and personal experience with sin. In this way most of the medieval
poet's themes were neglected or particularized. Only death retained
its generality, because its essential content was not defined by mutable
doctrines and tradition. The medieval poetic cosmos had pulled apart,
into various particular forms and a few general ones.

The generality of that cosmos also accounts for the second main
distinction of the short poems: their strangely firm, lucid, and at times
suggestive diction. The explanation for this, and the diction itself, are
simple: because the main words are relatively unmodified, and because
they tend to receive heavy stress accents, they stand out clearly and
sharply, like a few bright pebbles on the sand. This means that they
receive their full value; we can look at them carefully, "finger" them,
and get a sense of their weight and texture. This oddly verbal quality
is especially striking in poems that name exquisite things: "I syng of a
myden" (p. 83), "And By a chapell as y Came" (p. 119), "He bare hym
vp, he bare hym down" (p. 108), "Ther is no rose of swych vertu"
(p. 82), and "Maiden in the mor lay":

> Maiden in the mor lay—
> in the mor lay—
> seuenyst° fulle, seuenist fulle.   *seven nights*
> 4 Maiden in the mor lay—
> in the mor lay—
> seuenistes fulle ant a day.
>
> Welle° was hire mete.   *good*
> 8 wat was hire mete?
> þe primerole° ant the—   *primrose*
> þe primerole ant the—
> Welle was hire mete.
> 12 Wat was hire mete?
> the primerole ant the violet.

Welle [was hire dryng.°]   *drink*
wat was hire dryng?
16   [þe chelde° water of þe—]   *cold*
     [þe chelde water of þe—]
   [Welle was hire dryng.]
   [Wat was hire dryng?]
20   þe chelde water of þe welle-spring.

   Welle was hire bour.
   wat was hire bour?
     [þe rede rose an te—]
24   [þe rede rose an te—]
   [Welle was hire bour.]
   [Wat was hire bour?]
    þe rede rose an te lilie flour.

But it is also true of more homely poems that give us a palpable sense of words and things like ale, hawthorn, boar's heads, garlands, fire, bread, wine, snow, rain, and clouds, just as nursery rhymes tell us the truth about silver bells and cockleshells and Christmas pies. What J. R. R. Tolkien has said about fairy tales could be said as well about some of the medieval poems: "It was in fairy-stories that I first divined the potency of the words, and the wonder of the things, such as stone, and wood, and iron; tree and grass; house and fire; bread and wine."[11]

Finally, I would like to suggest an even more general basis for the "general" forms of Middle English lyrics. Among the eminent medievalists who have agreed about this general nature of medieval culture, Johan Huizinga has perhaps stated the thesis most fully and concisely:[12]

> Whatever the faculty of seeing specific traits may have been in the Middle Ages, it must be noted that men disregarded the individual qualities and fine distinctions of things, deliberately and of set purpose, in order always to bring them under some general principle. This mental tendency is a result of their profound idealism. People feel an imperious need of always and especially seeing the general sense, the connection with the absolute, the moral ideality, the ultimate significance of a thing. What is important is the impersonal. The mind is not in search of individual realities, but of models, examples, norms.

Huizinga goes on to illustrate this "mental tendency" with examples

138

drawn from many diverse cultural forms, and he speaks elsewhere of the medieval "craving to give a definite form to every idea." Is it purely fanciful, then, to see these tendencies not only in Middle English poems, but in the scholasticism, Gothic architecture, painting, and music of about the same period?

Corresponding to the firm structural outline of the short poem is the *manifestatio*, the highly explicit order and logic which Erwin Panofsky finds to be one of the "mental habits," or controlling principles, of both scholastic philosophy and Gothic architecture.[13] And Otto von Simson has thus described architectural drawings for Gothic cathedrals: "they appear like beautiful patterns of lines ordered according to geometrical principles."[14] Von Simson traces this mental habit to Saint Augustine's high regard for geometry, which, like music, can "lead the mind from the world of appearances to the contemplation of the divine order." Also, we find that British painting in the Middle Ages insisted on firm lines: "the fundamental characteristics of [medieval] English pictorial art in all its forms are not those of painting but of outline drawing, and the technique of manuscript illumination at its best is linear."[15] And late medieval music is straightforward and linear, compared to modern (not earlier medieval) music; even Machaut's *Messe de Nostre Dame* (c. 1364) consists of relatively few voices moving in clear melodic lines, unobscured by complex harmonies and dynamics.

Similarly, the denotative, sparsely modified nature of Middle English diction, its lack of nuances and fine connotations, corresponds to the even more strictly denotative language of the schoolmen; to the "Thin colour in bright or pale hues [which] might be added to enhance the line pattern in [medieval English] drawings, but rarely . . . completely obscure the line";[16] and to the lack of tone-color in late medieval music. For contrast, one need think only of Debussy, Renoir, and nearly any German philosopher of the last two hundred years. Even if the instruments had been available, it is impossible to conceive that "L'après-midi d'un Faune," Debussy's or Mallarmé's, could have been written in the fourteenth century. But *La Messe de Nostre Dame*, or something very much like it, could be written in the twentieth century, because history leaves many usable deposits, among which the various traditions—religious, philosophical, artistic—are preeminent. And anyone who learns the "rules of the game" can compose a fourteenth-century mass, or become a Catholic Christian, or write Middle English short poems.

Yf þou for luf receyued þys boke
Wher-on hit plesed þe to loke,
ffor crystys loue þat dyed on tre
Pray for hym þat gaf hit þe.

Reference Material

Notes

Chapter 1

1. My study is based mainly on the six standard collections which, according to R. H. Robbins, include nearly all short poems in Middle English "of any merit or historical interest" (see R. H. Robbins, rev. of R. T. Davies, *Medieval English Lyrics: A Critical Anthology* [London, 1963], *Speculum* 40 [1965]: 130).

2. J. V. Cunningham, *Tradition and Poetic Structure* (Denver, 1960), pp. 18–20.

3. René Wellek and Austin Warren, *Theory of Literature*, 3d ed. (New York, 1956), pp. 177–178.

4. Cunningham, p. 263. Cunningham elsewhere defines the uniqueness of verbal art and its interpretation: "For whatever be the case with the other arts, the arts of language consist of statements, and a statement means what it says. We look at what a work says to find out what it means, and the apprehension of its meaning is the work of art. Insofar as the meaning is not expressed in or not recoverable from the statements, the work is deficient. Furthermore, it is a simple principle of ethics, provable in daily conversation, that the meaning of a statement is not what anyone chances to attribute to it—how hurt we are when we are misconstrued—, but what it was intended to convey. The intention is the intention of the author as expressed in the language which he used and qualified by the circumstances under which he expressed it. Hence every statement is an historical statement, and it is properly understood only by historical interpretation" (p. 269).

5. Isabel C. Hungerland, *Poetic Discourse*, University of California Pubs. in Philosophy, 33 (Berkeley, 1958): 167.

6. Hungerland, p. 36.

7. Walter J. Ong, "The Jinnee in the Well-Wrought Urn," *Essays in Criticism* 4 (July 1954): 319.

8. The authors of the religious lyrics and most of the carols, if not the more worldly poems, were apparently clerics, who might be expected to remain anonymous on principle. See two studies by Rossell Hope Robbins: "The Authors of the Middle English Religious Lyrics," *JEGP* 39 (1940): 230–238, in which he argues that the Franciscans were especially important as religious poets; and "Middle English Carols as Processional Hymns," *SP* 56 (1959): 559–582.

9. Kemp Malone and Albert C. Baugh, *The Middle Ages*, Vol. I in *A Literary History of England*, ed. Albert C. Baugh, 2d ed. (New York, 1967), pp. 114–115. All subsequent references to Baugh are to pp. 114–115.

143

10. For an exhaustive list of rhetorical figures in the thirteenth-century lyric, see Alexander Müller, *Mittelenglische Geistliche und Weltliche Lyrik des XIII. Jahrhunderts: nach Motiven und Formen* (Halle, 1911). Müller's conclusion is also valid for the lyrics of the fourteenth and fifteenth centuries: "allgemein betrachtet, hat die weltliche Lyrik formell und stylistisch manches mit der geistlichen Lyrik gemeinsam, die Hauptabweichung besteht in der Verwendung der Motive" (p. 134).

11. James J. Murphy, "A New Look at Chaucer and the Rhetoricians," *RES* 15 (1964): 2. The main classical sources of medieval rhetoric are Cicero's *De inventione*, the *De rhetorica ad Herennium*, and the Epistle of Horace to Piso.

12. David Knowles, *The Evolution of Medieval Thought* (London, 1963), pp. 84–86.

13. James J. Murphy, "The Arts of Discourse, 1050–1400," *MedStud* 23 (1961): 198: "The primer itself—Donatus—describes even more tropes than Vinsauf does; and the next most popular elementary text (the *Graecismus* of Evrard of Béthune) treats some hundred *figurae*, the *Doctrinale* of Alexandre de Villedieu seventy-eight."

14. Murphy, *RES* 15: 16.

Chapter 2

1. From the preface to *The Picture of Dorian Gray* (New York, 1960), p. 6.

2. Ruskin emphasizes the medieval artisan's freedom to contribute something of his own while remaining subordinate: "This is the glory of Gothic architecture, that every jot and tittle, every point and niche of it, affords room, fuel, and focus for individual fire. But you cease to acknowledge this, and you refuse to accept the help of the lesser mind, if you require the work to be all executed in a great manner. Your business is to think out all of it nobly. . . . the mind of the inferior workman is recognized, and has full room for action, but is guided and ennobled by the ruling mind" (*The Stones of Venice*, Vol. IX of *The Complete Works of John Ruskin*, ed. E. T. Cook and Alexander Wedderburn [London, 1903], I, 291). Though the analogy should not be pressed too far, the architect is to the masons somewhat as the theologian is to the religious poets.

3. 14/15th, introduction, pp. xvii–xviii. Much of the following is based on this introduction, which lucidly sets forth all the necessary facts about poets and manuscripts.

4. 13th, introduction, pp. xxxvi and xxxvii: "We know that minstrels frequently visited religious houses, and no doubt they entertained their hosts with songs from their repertory. Through the gates of the monasteries passed also itinerant friars and *clerici vagantas*. It would have been an easy matter, then, for a monastic collector to gather from a wide field the materials which are here assembled, and it seems safer [than regarding Harley 2253 as a

monk's poetic autobiography] to regard the Harley MS as representing the attempt of a collector with an unusually catholic interest in literature to transcribe poems which he found in written form and also to write down songs which he heard."

5. Rossell Hope Robbins, "Middle English Carols as Processional Hymns," *SP* 56 (1959): 561 and 582: "The carols are obviously intended for a definitely practical religious use: they form a means to salvation just as surely as the liturgy, hymns, or private prayers. . . in many carols are prayer-tags and popular prayers, Biblical and sometimes patristic references, and Latin lines from hymns and antiphons. . . . [The carol's] main tradition was not vernacular, secular, and foreign; but Latin, religious, and native." The carol consists of quatrains with refrain, and a two-line burden sung before the first and after each stanza.

6. See Rossell Hope Robbins, "The Earliest Carols and the Franciscans," *MLN* 53 (1938): 239–245.

7. Quoted in 14/15th, p. xxiii.

8. Sylvia L. Thrupp, *The Merchant Class of Medieval London*, p. 158: "If 40 per cent of the lay male Londoners of this period [1467–1476] could read Latin, it is a fair guess that some 50 per cent could read English."

9. H. J. Chaytor, *From Script to Print*, p. 17: "The hired *scriptor* or scrivener began to supplement or to replace the monastic scribe at an early date; St. Albans made regulations for the employment of such professionals before the middle of the thirteenth century; in the late fourteenth century the York scriveners formed a guild of their own. In university towns the scrivener could make a steady income; those who were under university control were occupied with books on law, theology or medicine, and authors of *belles-lettres* had to content themselves with scriveners not thus occupied, who were less reliable than the more professional class."

10. H. S. Bennett, *Chaucer and the Fifteenth Century*, p. 116: "There are extant enough manuscripts written by Shirley, or partly copied from his work, for us to realize that they were compiled to satisfy an existing public; and these manuscripts contain not single pieces but a number of items to satisfy a variety of tastes." "Aureate Collection" is Robbins' term for manuscripts written in a Latinate, "noble" style to suit their noble readers (14/15th: xxii–xxiv).

11. Walter F. Schirmer, "Dichter und Publikum zu Ende des 15. Jahrhunderts in England," *Zeitschrift für Ästhetik und Allgemeine Kunstwissenschaft* 28 (1934): 217: "Für die Literatur heisst das [the War of the Roses] die Vernichtung des Publikums. . . . Die vielen anonymen kleinen Stücke . . . verzichten dann ganz auf eine Widmung."

12. Rossell Hope Robbins, "Wall Verses at Launceston Priory," *Archiv für das Studium der Neueren Sprachen und Literaturen* 200 (1963): 338–343. Among the verses found on walls are two charming epigrams from the dining hall (*aula*) of Launceston Priory; they were placed above the tables of the

servants, and, like the presence of the tables themselves, were designed to keep each servant firmly in his particular place (p. 342):

A. *Supra tabulam valettorum*   *Above the Table of the Servants*
    Whoso loueth wel to fare
    Euer spende and neuer spare
    But he haue the more good   *Unless he has the more goods*
    His heer wol growe thurgh his hood[a]

B. *Super tabulam garcionum et operariorum*[b]
    In anoþer mannes hous
    Ne be þou neuer coueytous
    Miche° desire for to haue   *Much*
    ffor þat is þe condicione of a knaue

[a] (i.e., the hood will fall apart as a result of poverty)
[b] *Above the Table of the Chamber-Grooms and Workmen*

Both of these poems had been copied into an early fifteenth century manuscript.

13. See William Edward Mead, *The English Medieval Feast* (London, 1931), p. 16: "The intimate connection between the Church and the social life of the Middle Ages is obvious at every turn; and although the religious element is in many cases far from obtrusive in the actual feasts, the mere fact that a day was set apart as a church holiday often determined its selection as a fitting time for a banquet." Thus the occasion for a festive poem is closely related to the occasion and purpose of the feast.

14. Of course historical scholarship is not always concerned with trends and statistics and other very general matters; it can also evoke the "historical sensation" or "contact" that Johan Huizinga has described: "It is not an aesthetic enjoyment, a religious emotion, an awe of nature, a metaphysical recognition—and yet it is a figure in this series. The object of the sensation is not human figures in their individual form, not human lives or human thoughts one thinks one can disentangle. What the mind creates or experiences in this connection can hardly be called an image. If and insofar as it assumes a form, it is one that remains complex and vague: an *Ahnung* just as much of roads and houses and fields, of sounds and colors, as of stimulated and stimulating people. This contact with the past, which is accompanied by an utter conviction of genuineness and truth, can be evoked by a line from a document or a chronicle, by a print, by a few notes of an old song. It is not an element that the writer infuses in his work by using certain words. It lies beyond the book of history, not in it. The reader brings it to the writer, it is his response to the writer's call" (*Men and Ideas* [New York, 1959], p. 54).

15. See V. A. Kolve, *The Play Called Corpus Christi* (Stanford, 1966), p. 162: "Medieval fasting was, furthermore, very severe, forbidding all flesh, including 'melted' flesh (butter, milk, cheese) and all fowl."

16. John R. H. Moorman, *Church Life in England in the Thirteenth Century* (Cambridge, 1946), p. 175.

17. A. R. Myers, *England in the Late Middle Ages*, rev. ed. Penguin Books, (Harmondsworth, Middlesex, 1956), p. 209.

18. According to records of Richard Swinfield's household expenses for 1289–1290, "the actual amount consumed on Easter Day was 1½ carcases of salt beef, 1¾ carcases of fresh beef, 5 pigs, 4½ calves, 22 kids, 3 fat deer, 12 capons, 88 pigeons and 1400 eggs, besides bread and cheese, beer without stint, and 66 gallons of Bosbury wine" (quoted in Moorman, p. 178).

19. Ed. E. V. Gordon and J. R. R. Tolkien; 2d ed. edited by Norman Davis (Oxford, 1968). For an extremely full, valuable description of dining and minstrelsy in the medieval hall, see Urban Tigner Holmes, *Daily Living in the Twelfth Century* (Madison, 1964), pp. 87–91 (dinner) and 215–219 (minstrelsy).

20. Robbins glosses "Verse le bauere" with " 'Pour out the drink'? Or *vesse* [sic] = voiçi?" (p. 231), but the former seems more likely, since it would be the third in a parallel series of four transitive, imperative verbs.

21. C. S. Lewis, in *Studies in Medieval and Renaissance Literature* (Cambridge, 1966), offers a fine explanation of medieval pageantry and celebration: "A modern mind will of course say that the men of that age fashioned heaven in the likeness of Earth and, because they like high pomps, the Mass, coronations, pageants, tournaments, carols, attributed such activities *par excellence* to the translunary world. But remember that they thought it was the other way round. They thought that the ecclesiastical hierarchy and the social hierarchy on Earth were dim reproductions of the celestial hierarchies. The pageantry and ceremony which they indulged in to the utmost of their powers were their attempt to imitate the *modus operandi* of the universe; to live, in that sense, 'according to nature'. That is why so much medieval art and literature is concerned simply with asserting the nature of things. They like to tell, and to be told again and again, about the universe I have been describing" (p. 60).

22. See 15th, p. 318, n. on No. 79.

23. J. V. Cunningham, *The Exclusions of a Rhyme* (Denver, 1960), p. 22.

24. This aesthetic theory, which Schiller derived from Kant, and which originally described the "uselessness" of art, has been applied by the German Thomist Josef Pieper to feasting (and secondarily to art). See *Zustimmung zur Welt: Eine Theorie des Festes* (Munich, 1963): "Ein Fest feiern heisst nämlich zweifellos so viel wie etwas tun, das aus jeder denkbaren Beziehung auf fremde Zwecke und aus allem, damit' und, um zu' herausgekommen ist. . . . [es ist] eine in sich selbst sinnvolle Tätigkeit" (p. 23); "Indem einer die Arbeitsruhe des Feiertags verwirklicht und bejaht, verzichtet er auf den Ertrag eines Arbeitstages. . . . Was geschieht, ist nicht nur keine Nutzung; es ist etwas von der Art des Opfers und also das äusserste Gegenteil von Nutzung, das überhaupt gedacht werden kann" (p. 36).

25. 14/15th, p. 258, n. on No. 94.

26. This normally occurs in portrayals of the Last Judgment. See *The Chester Plays*, ed. Matthews, EETS, E.S. 115 (Oxford, 1916), pt. ii, 441–442, stanzas 50–52; and Emile Mâle, *The Gothic Image: Religious Art in France of the Thirteenth Century*, trans. Dora Nussey (New York, 1958), p. 369 (Mâle is discussing the Last Judgment at Chartres): "With a fine gesture He lifts His wounded hands, and through the open garment is seen the wound in His side. . . . One feels that He has not yet spoken to the world, and the fateful silence is terrible. His significant gesture is explained by the doctors. 'He shows His wounds', says one of them, 'to bear witness to the truth of the gospel and to prove that He was in truth crucified for us' [quoted from Vincent of Beauvais, *Speculum historiale. Epilog. Tractatus de ultimis temporibus* (Douai, 1624), cxii]."

27. According to George J. Engelhardt, "the text of the *contemptus mundi* in the Christian tradition" is I John 2:15–18 (quoted from the New Jerusalem Bible): "You must not love this passing world or anything that is in the world. The love of the Father cannot be in any man who loves the world, because nothing the world has to offer—the sensual body, the lustful eye, pride in possessions—could ever come from the Father but only from the world; and the world, with all it craves for, is coming to an end; but anyone who does the will of God remains for ever. Children, these are the last days; you were told that an Antichrist must come, and now several antichrists have already appeared; we know from this that these are the last days" ("The *De contemptu mundi* of Bernardus Morvalensis, Part One: A Study on Commonplace," *MedStud*, 22 [1960]: 135). See Rainer Rudolf, *Ars Moriendi: von der Kunst des Heilsamen Lebens und Sterbens* (Cologne, 1957), pp. 25–26: "Eine besonders wirkungsvolle Art der 'Kunst des heilsamen Lebens' war es von den Anfängen der christlichen Literatur an, die Reize der menschlichen Schönheit zu erbaulichen Zwecken oder von einem höheren theologischen Standpunkt aus als nichtig oder wertlos hinzustellen und die Vergänglichkeit aller irdischen Güter nachdrücklich zu betonen. . . . Zu den ältesten Werken dieser Art gehört der pseudoagustinische *Sermo de contemptu mundi* [. . . and a work written around 427 by Bishop Eucherius of Lyons]."

28. See especially Johan H. Huizinga, "The Vision of Death," Chap. 11 of *The Waning of the Middle Ages* (New York, 1954).

29. G. R. Owst, *Preaching in Medieval England* (Cambridge, 1926), p. 340.

30. R. W. Ackerman, "*The Debate of the Body and Soul* and Parochial Christianity," *Speculum* 37 (1962): 546.

31. In his note on this poem, Robbins says "Here the poet is trying to represent the emotions of a drunken man, who wants everything to stand still; then, when he trips, is able to relax his body" (p. 265). But Robbins himself glosses "tryp" in "When ye tryp and daunce" (14/15th: 211,l. 48) as "dance," and "trippyng" in "by trippyng & by dauncing" (14/15th:28, l. 39) as "dancing" (see the entry under "trippede," p. 322). And the phrase "trippe a lutel wit þi fot" seems to be an imperative, parallel to "stondet alle stille."

32. W. B. Yeats, *Essays and Introductions* (London, 1961), p. 521: "I tried to make the language of poetry coincide with that of passionate, normal speech."

33. Ezra Pound, *Personae* (New York, 1926), p. 31.

34. Quoted in R. W. Southern, *The Making of the Middle Ages* (New Haven, 1953), p. 233. For the origins of this "Franciscan" devotion, see pp. 226–240.

35. Later in the Middle Ages, poets and painters tended to lose sight of their spiritual goal and became absorbed in sensual details per se. See Theodor Wolpers, "Geschichte der englischen Marienlyrik," *Anglia* 6 (1950): 3–88. The poets frequently celebrated the beauty of various parts of Mary's body.

36. The same quality of feeling for these scenes appears in the visual arts of the period (Southern, pp. 237–238): "Until [the late eleventh century], the most powerful representations of the Crucifixion in Western Europe had expressed the sense of that remote and majestic act of Divine power which had filled the minds of earlier generations. But a change had been slowly creeping in, which led in time to the realization of the extreme limits of human suffering: the dying figure was stripped of its garments, the arms sagged with the weight of the body, the head hung on one side, the eyes were closed, the blood ran down the Cross. . . . In the eleventh century, the West had long been familiar with the child seated as if enthroned on his Mother's knee, holding up his right hand in benediction and, in his left, clasping a Book, the symbol of wisdom, or an orb, the symbol of dominion. This conception persisted and was never abandoned, but it was joined by many other forms which expressed the more intimate inclinations of later medieval piety, such as the laughing Child, the Child playing with an apple or a ball, the Child caressing its Mother, or the Child being fed from its Mother's breast." See also Chapter 3, n. 11.

37. See Rosemary Woolf, "The Theme of Christ the lover-knight in medieval English literature," *RES*, N.S. 13 (1962): 1–16.

38. R. T. Davies comments on "Alysoun": "The description of the beloved is the traditional ideal, the poet's sufferings are those of countless others . . . and the eloquent comparison in line 30 is found, e.g., in [13th: 51], l. 151" (*Medieval English Lyrics* [Northwestern University Press, 1967], p. 313). For a concise discussion of courtly love, see G. L. Brook, ed., *The Harley Lyrics: the Middle English Lyrics of MS. Harley 2253*, 2d ed. (Manchester, 1955), pp. 8–14.

For a more extended discussion, see C. S. Lewis, *The Allegory of Love* (Oxford, 1958), Chap. 1. Lewis conveniently summarizes courtly love as it appears in troubadour poetry: "The sentiment, of course, is love, but love of a highly specialized sort, whose characteristics may be enumerated as Humility, Courtesy, Adultery and the Religion of Love. The lover is always abject. Obedience to his lady's lightest wish, however whimsical, and silent acquiescence in her rebukes, however unjust, are the only virtues he dares to claim. There is a service of love closely modelled on the service which a feudal vassal owes to his lord. The lover is the lady's 'man.' " The English courtly lyrics derive mainly from the tradition of northern France, which is more physical and less self-abasing: sexual intercourse is encouraged, and love must be mutual.

39. See G. G. Coulton, *The Medieval Panorama* (Cleveland, 1962), pp. 614–628, and Francis Lee Utley, *The Crooked Rib* (Columbus, 1944), pp. 3–38. John Jay Parry, in his introduction to Andreas Capellanus' *Art of Courtly Love* (New York, 1964), gives a nutshell history of antifeminism in medieval thought: "Eve's sin was generally looked upon as the cause of the downfall of mankind, for without it Adam would not have sinned; Solomon was unable to find a good woman; Paul held that it was good for a man not to touch a woman, and so forth. . . . The early Fathers of the Church taught that virginity was preferable to marriage and attempted to popularize the celibate life by dwelling on the vices of women. St. Jerome, for example, angered by Jovinian's statement that, other things being equal, a virgin was no better in the sight of God than a wife or a widow, attempted to prove him wrong and so provided the Middle Ages with a convenient compendium of antifeminist literature. Probably there was no age that did not furnish such attacks upon women, but in the period just before Andreas wrote [c. 1185] they seem to have been especially numerous" (p. 18, including n. 58).

40. 13th, p. xx.

41. *Poems and Prose of Gerard Manley Hopkins*, selected by W. H. Gardner (London, 1954), p. 60.

42. *The Note-Books and Papers of Gerard Manley Hopkins*, ed. Humphry House (London, 1937), pp. 309–310. Also found in the convenient but incomplete Penguin selection (see note 41), p. 148.

Chapter 3

1. See Josephine Miles, *Eras and Modes in English Poetry* (Berkeley, 1957), pp. 15 ff.

2. See R. L. Greene, " 'The Port of Peace': Not Death [as identified by Carleton Brown] but God," *MLN* 69 (1954): 307–309. Greene points out that the poem is a translation, done in 1410 by a certain John Walton, of Meter 10 from Book III of Boethius' *Consolation*.

3. Donald Davie, in a discussion of Fenollosa's influence on Ezra Pound, describes a modern poetic which is almost point for point the precise opposite of Middle English verse practice: "[Fenollosa] delivers a number of precepts: that the good poet will use, wherever possible, the full sentence driving through a transitive verb; that he will avoid, wherever possible, the copula; that he will rearrange, wherever possible, negations, so as to use a positive verb of negation; that he will avoid intransitive verbs; that he will be fond of verbs and cut down as far as possible the use of other parts of speech; that when he uses an abstract word he will draw attention, by his use of it,

to its etymological growth out of concrete actions; that in using parts of speech other than verbs he will choose wherever possible words that reveal in themselves verbal elements or origins" (*Articulate Energy: an Inquiry into the Syntax of English Poetry* [London, 1955], p. 39).

4. See Otto von Simson, *The Gothic Cathedral: Origins of Gothic Architecture and the Medieval Concept of Order* (New York, 1962), pp. 50–51: "For the twelfth and thirteenth centuries light was the source and essence of all visual beauty. Thinkers who differ as widely as do Hugh of St. Victor and Thomas Aquinas both ascribe to the beautiful two main characteristics: consonance of parts, or proportion, and luminosity. The stars, gold, and precious stones are called beautiful because of this quality. In the philosophical literature of the time, as in the courtly epic, no attributes are used more frequently to describe visual beauty than 'lucid', 'luminous', 'clear.'" (Von Simson provides abundant references.)

5. Richard Wilbur, *The Poems of Richard Wilbur* (New York, 1963), p. 137.

6. W. Bedell Stanford, *Greek Metaphor: Studies in Theory and Practice* (Oxford, 1936), pp. 9–10.

7. Winifred Nowottny, *The Language Poets Use* (London, 1965), p. 60.

8. Wallace Stevens, *The Collected Works of Wallace Stevens* (New York, 1957), p. 67.

9. I have chosen these lines mainly because they have been analyzed very subtly in context: see Yvor Winters, *In Defense of Reason*, 3d ed. (Denver, 1947), p. 447.

10. R. T. Davies includes a valuable appendix on "Types and Titles of the Blessed Virgin Mary" used in the poems (*Medieval English Lyrics*, pp. 371–378). The following are especially relevant: Burning Bush (of Sinai), Dove, Earth (untilled), Fountain-Well-Spring (sealed, shut up), Gem(s), Lamp, Light, Lily among thorns, Medicine, Mirror without spot, Rose in Jericho (without thorns), Shield, Star (of the sea, of bliss, etc.), Throne (of Solomon, of God).

11. See, for example, R. L. Greene's summary of the Franciscan influence on English carols: "The tempering of the austerity of Christianity by the appeal to tender emotion and personal love for Christ, the invocation of pity for His sorrow in the cradle and suffering on the cross, which is particularly to be noted in the lullaby and Crucifixion carols, are part of the legacy of Francis to the centuries which followed his ministry. An excellent expression of this religious attitude is to be found in the *Meditationes Vitae Christi.* . . . The emphasis which it lays upon the humanity of Christ, the suffering which He underwent, and the duty of the Christian to feel compassion for Him is strikingly similar to a corresponding emphasis in some of the carols. The religion informing most of the sacred carols is in large measure a Franciscan Christianity" (*Carols*, p. cxxvii). See also p. [29].

12. *Personae*, p. 141.

13. See Moorman, pp. 144–145.

14. "Wode-gore" occurs in 13th: 85, l. 31. Brown glosses it as "forest plot," but he also glosses "gore" in "So godlich ounder gore" (13th: 51, l. 149) as "clothing." And the "forest-clothing" must surely refer to the leaves, a reading which makes good sense in context ("vnder þe wode-gore").

15. Stevens, p. 27.

16. See Abrams, p. 95: "Some symbols are 'conventional,' or 'public'; thus 'the Cross,' 'the Red, White, and Blue,' 'the Good Shepherd' are terms that signify objects of which the symbolic meanings are widely known." The hawks and hounds were not as familiar as the Cross, but they were of the same order.

17. The interrelated vices or virtues are often presented as the interrelated parts of a tree. For a discussion of this technique, see Robert W. Ackerman, *Backgrounds to Medieval English Literature* (New York, 1966), pp. 95–97.

18. Other examples may be found in 14/15th: 7, 30, and 95; 13th: 48, stanzas 6–8; and 15th: 100.

19. See Stephen Manning, *Wisdom and Number: Toward a Critical Appraisal of the Middle English Lyric* (Lincoln, Nebr., 1962), p. 113. Manning distinguishes here between arbitrary allegory, in which "the vehicle bears no relationship whatever to the tenor: and descriptive allegory, in which the two terms of the comparison are intrinsically alike."

20. Hart Crane, *The Complete Poems of Hart Crane* (New York, 1958), p. 84.

21. See Edmund Reiss, "A Critical Approach to the Middle English Lyric," *College English* 27 (1966): 373–379. Reiss sees all the implications of the puns except that Christ, like the sun, will also rise (in "Nou goth sonne vnder wod," 13th: 1). But I am not persuaded that the horn in "Wel, qwa sal thir hornes blau" (LL, p. 187) suggests Judgment Day (p. 378), since there is no doubt who will blow the horn on that occasion (the dead person in the poem is not the Archangel Gabriel). And Reiss's eccentric scansion leads him to some over-ingenious readings: he scans "Foweles in the frith" (13th: 8) as 2-2-4-2-3, whereas it seems clearly to be written in a very regular trimeter (the only inversion is the first foot of the first line). As a result of this scansion, Reiss does not notice that "with" in the fourth line receives a (relatively) heavy stress, and he argues thus: "After stressed *walke* appears an unaccented syllable, giving the line the impression of stumbling and thereby reflecting the narrator's state of mind" (p. 377).

22. David Halliburton has shown that "peerless" is the primary meaning of "makeles," that "mateless" is a secondary meaning, and that the word could not mean "without husband" since Mary was, after all, married to Joseph. But in spite of Halliburton's careful arguments, there is no doubt that *make*, in Middle English, means "mate, consort . . . husband or wife, lover or mistress" (Shorter *Oxford English Dictionary*) and that *les* means "without." "Makeles" must therefore have the secondary meaning of "mateless" in the sense of "without a sexual companion." This is quite appropriate,

inasmuch as the poem describes how Christ was conceived and ends by stressing Mary's unique, well known qualification for being God's mother: "moder & mayden was neuer non but che—/ wel may *swych* a lady godes moder be" (emphasis mine). See David G. Halliburton, "The Myden Makeles," in *Papers on Language and Literature* 4 (Spring 1968): 115–120.

23. The Christmas season lasted either for twelve days, till Epiphany, or for the full forty days to the Purification. "Both traditions flourish in popular custom, some communities of England removing Christmas greens, for instance, after Twelfth Night, others leaving them until Candlemas" (*Carols*, p. 354, n. on No. 7).

24. *The Shorter Oxford English Dictionary*, prepared by William Little, H. W. Fowler, and J. Coulson, rev. and ed. C. T. Onions; 3d ed., rev. with addenda (Oxford, 1959).

25. See Huizinga, *The Waning of the Middle Ages*, pp. 228–229: "In the Middle Ages everyone liked to base a serious argument on a text, so as to give it a foundation. . . . The tendency to give each particular case the character of a moral sentence or of an example, so that it becomes something substantiated and unchallengeable, the crystallization of thought, in short, finds its most general and natural expression in the proverb."

26. Ernst Robert Curtius, *European Literature and the Latin Middle Ages*, trans. Willard R. Trask (New York, 1963), p. 70.

27. Hopkins, *Poems and Prose*, p. 50.

28. Nowottny, p. 60.

29. Nowottny, p. 67.

30. See Chapter 2. Other students of the lyrics have also noticed the thinness of figurative language. See Sr. M. Theresa Clare Hogan, "A Critical Study of the Middle English Lyrics of Br. Museum MS. Harley 2253," *DA* 23 (1962): 1350: "The imagery [figurative language] of the Middle English poems is rather limited, being confined generally to passages of actual description and to metaphors repeated indiscriminately in verses of didacticism, of religious and profane love"; and the unpublished M.A. thesis (Stanford, 1962) by Jane L. Curry, "Imagery in the Middle English Secular Lyric: The Love Lyric," pp. 32 ff. (there is little metaphor) and p. 36 (there is not much personification, allegory, and symbolism before 1400).

31. See Fred C. Robinson, "The Significance of Names in Old English Literature," *Anglia* 82 (1968): 14–58. Robinson shows that such titles as Star of the Sea (for Mary) are literal etymologies of the proper names, based on Saint Jerome's linguistic methods of interpreting Scripture: "One result of the [patristic] commentators' onomastic zeal was that many names came to have multiple etymologies, any or all of which might become starting points for spiritual interpretations. . . . The name *Mary*, for example, acquired a host of interpretations among Latin commentators—*stella maris, domina, dominatrix, illuminatrix. . .*" (p. 21). Robinson's conclusions apply to writings in Middle English as well as Old English.

Chapter 4

1. Harry Caplan, trans., *Rhetorica Ad Herennium* (Cambridge, Mass., 1954), pp. 252–253:

> *Sunt igitur tria genera, quae genera nos figuras appellamus, in quibus omnis oratio non vitiosa consumitur: unam gravem, alteram mediocrem, tertiam extenuatam vocamus. Gravis est quae constat ex verborum gravium levi et ornata constructione. Mediocris est quae constat ex humiliore neque tamen ex infima et pervulgatissima verborum dignitate. Adtenuata est quae demissa est usque ad usitatissimam puri consuetudinem sermonis.*

2. Edmond Faral, *Les Arts Poétiques du XIIe et du XIIIe Siècle* (Paris, 1958), p. 312:

> *Sunt igitur tres styli, humilis, mediocris, grandiloquus. Et tales recipiunt appellationes styli ratione personarum vel rerum de quibus fit tractatus. Quando enim de generalibus personis vel rebus tractatur, tunc est stylus grandiloquus; quando de humilibus, humilis; quando de mediocris, mediocris. Quolibet stylo utitur Virgilius: in* Bucolicis *humili, in* Georgicis *mediocri, in* Eneyde *grandiloquo.*

3. Charles Muscatine, *Chaucer and the French Tradition* (Berkeley, 1964), p. 59.

4. Muscatine, p. 17.

5. *The Exeter Book*, ed. George Philip Krapp and Elliott Van Kirk Dobbie (New York, 1936), pp. 136–137.

6. Theo Stemmler has shown conclusively that Charles D'Orléans could not have written the English poems traditionally ascribed to him. Stemmler suggests that the English lyrics, which are free rather than literal translations from the French of Charles D'Orléans, were written by a single anonymous poet, probably a minstrel, who had a good but incomplete knowledge of French. See "Zur Verfasserfrage der Charles D'Orleans zugeschriebenen englischen Gedichte," *Anglia* 82 (1964): 458–473.

7. See Otto Jospersen, *Growth and Structure of the English Language*, 9th ed. (New York, 1956), p. 92. The light rhythms also add to the elegance.

8. From "Evening Without Angels," *Collected Poems of Wallace Stevens*, p. 137.

9. See, for example, John C. Mendenhall, *Aureate Terms: A Study in the Literary Diction of the Fifteenth Century* (Lancaster, Pa., 1919), and John Allen Conley, "Four Studies in Aureate Terms," unpublished dissertation (Stanford, 1956–1957).

10. See Jespersen, pp. 148–156 (for a brief summary, pp. 155–156).

11. For an excellent discussion, see Leo Spitzer, *"Explication de Texte* Applied to Three Great Middle English Poems," *Archivum Linguisticum* 3 (1949): 152 ff.

Chapter 5

1. Yvor Winters, *Collected Poems* (Denver, 1960), p. 63.

2. See Jacob Schipper, *History of English Versification* (Oxford, 1910), p. 126; and C. S. Lewis, "The Fifteenth-Century Heroic Line," *Essays and Studies by Members of the English Association* 24 (1938): 28 ff.

3. In *New Poets of England and America*, ed. Donald Hall, Robert Pack, and Louis Simpson (New York, 1957), p. 54.

4. Manning, *Wisdom and Number*, p. vii.

5. *Tradition and Poetic Structure*, pp. 38–39. The whole concluding paragraph is highly relevant to this study:

> In the course of this paper six characteristics of one kind of poetry have been discriminated and opposed to six characteristics of another kind. The one employs a complex and modulated metre; the other an obvious metre conforming to a simple mathematical scheme. The one plays the syntactical structure against the metrical line; the other shows a marked coincidence of the two. In the one tradition the length of the poem tends to be a free determination; in the other it tends to be fixed and given. The outline of thought in the one tends not to correspond to the units of the external form; in the other it tends to correspond. The paraphrasable meaning of the one is largely implicit and to be inferred from the text; with the other it is explicit. Finally, the conceptual basis of the first kind of poetry will tend to be one of continuity and degree; in the second kind it will tend to be one of discontinuity, identity, and contradiction. The first kind is exemplified by the poetry of Horace, Vergil, and Statius, by Milton's *Lycidas* and most of his sonnets, and by a great deal of more modern poetry. The second kind is exemplified in most medieval and Tudor lyric. The first may be called the classical method, the second the medieval, and the history of the English lyric may be construed in terms of the transition from the second to the first.

6. *Articulate Energy*, p. 67.

7. Robbins prints Beatrice Geary's convenient table of statistics in 14/15th: p. xlix (note that Miss Geary "excluded, for example, versions of the Paternoster and Ave Maria, a fact which accounts for the small number of couplets in her tabulation").

8. Alexander Pope, *Minor Poems*, Vol. VI of the Twickenham Edition, ed. Norman Ault and John Butt (New Haven, 1954), p. 372.

Chapter 6

1. Winters and Cunningham are the most persuasive admirers of these poems. See, for example, *In Defense of Reason*, p. 31, and "Logic and Lyric; Marvell, Dunbar, and Nashe" in *Tradition and Poetic Structure*, pp. 40–58.

2. For a convenient discussion, with further references, of the French Feast of Fools, see Kolve, *The Play Called Corpus Christi* (Stanford, 1966), pp. 135–137: "for example, Beauvais service books indicate a drinking bout on the church porch, censing with pudding and sausage, introducing a live ass into the church, and using a specially written *ordinale* where parts of the Mass ended with brays and were answered with braying responses from the congregation."

3. *The Oxford Nursery Rhyme Book*, assembled by Iona and Peter Opie (Oxford, 1963), p. 62.

4. Manning, p. 57. Manning lists five main types of religious form: (1) [e.g., "In a tabernacle of a toure," 14th: 132] ... "structured on a definite sequence in the spiritual life" (p. 59); (2) "the liturgical formula of address plus petition. ... Not progression but sheer force of repetition gives such a poem structure" (p. 62); (3) "meditation" [mental picturing of the scene accompanied by pious emotions, petition, etc.] (p. 72); (4) "Devotion to the five joys of Mary, which bears a structural relationship to the meditation" (p. 74); (5) [meditation combined with debate] (p. 77).

5. John Crowe Ransom, *Poems and Essays* (New York, 1955), p. 37.

6. I mean such practical allegories as may be found in popular religious manuals and treatises (the *Livre de Seyntz Medicines*, *The Desert of Religion*, and others). See Ackerman, *Backgrounds*, pp. 89, 93–97, and Pantin, pp. 189–243 *passim*.

7. For a lucid *explication de texte*, see Leo Spitzer, "*Explication de Texte* Applied to Three Great Middle English Poems," *Archivum Linguisticum* 3(1949): p. 137 ff.

Chapter 7

1. Carl von Kraus, ed., *Die Gedichte Walthers von der Vogelweide* (Berlin, 1959), p. 37: "Ich hân mîn lêhen, al die werlt, ich hân mîn lêhen. / nû enfürhte ich niht den hornunc an die zêhen ... ich bin ze lange arm gewesen ân mînen danc. / ich was sô voller scheltens daz mîn âten stanc. ..." The next two Walther poems, "Owê war sint verswunden" and "Under der linden," can be found, in spite of the book's extraordinary index, on pages 170 and 52, respectively, of this standard edition.

2. The poems discussed in this paragraph can be found in *Lyrik des Späten Mittelalters,* ed. Hermann Maschek (Leipzig, 1939).

3. The critical edition of the *Carmina Burana* is that of A. Hilka and O. Schumann (Heidelberg, 1941), but this poem and the Archpoet's "Confession" are printed in the more convenient *Penguin Book of Latin Verse,* ed. Frederick Brittain (Harmondsworth, 1962), pp. 267, 206.

4. The poems discussed in this paragraph can be found in *To the Fifteenth Century,* Vol. I of *The Penguin Book of French Verse,* ed. Brian Woledge (Harmondsworth 1961).

5. The standard edition of Villon is *François Villon, Oeuvres,* ed. A. Longnon and L. Foulet (Paris, 4th ed., 1932), in the series *Les Classiques Français du Moyen Age.* A more convenient edition is Bantam Books' *The Complete Works of François Villon,* with a facing translation by Anthony Bonner (New York, 1960); this poem is on p. 160.

6. See Doris Mary Stenton, *English Society in the Early Middle Ages (1066–1307),* Penguin Books, (Harmondsworth, 1955). Lady Stenton quotes a description of King Stephen by Walter Map, a near-contemporary: "Of outstanding skill in arms, but in other things almost an idiot, except that he was more inclined towards evil" (p. 33).

7. Elliott V. K. Dobbie, ed., *The Anglo-Saxon Minor Poems,* Vol. VI of *The Anglo-Saxon Poetic Records* (New York, 1931–1953), p. 55.

8. Wesley Trimpi, "Jonson and the Native Tradition of the Plain Style," Chap. 6, *Ben Jonson's Poems: A Study of the Plain Style* (Stanford, 1962).

9. Kenneth Muir, ed., *The Collected Poems of Sir Thomas Wyatt* (London, 1960), p. 150.

10. Agnes Latham, ed., *The Poems of Sir Walter Raleigh* (London, 1962), p. 51. The next two poems by Raleigh ("Three things there bee" and "The Lie") are on pp. 49 and 45, respectively.

11. J. R. R. Tolkien, *Tree and Leaf* (London, 1964), p. 53.

12. Huizinga, *The Waning of the Middle Ages,* pp. 215–216, 248.

13. See Erwin Panofsky, *Gothic Architecture and Scholasticism* (Cleveland, 1957), pp. 21, 30, 34–36, 58.

14. Von Simson, *The Gothic Cathedral,* pp. 13, 22.

15. Margaret Rickert, *Painting in Britain: The Middle Ages* (London, 1954), p. 217.

16. Rickert, p. 2.

Selected Bibliography

1. Texts of the Lyrics

Brook, G. L., ed. *The Harley Lyrics: The Middle English Lyrics of Ms. Harley 2253.* 2nd ed. Manchester, 1955.

Brown, Carleton, ed. *English Lyrics of the Thirteenth Century.* Oxford, 1932.

———, ed. *Religious Lyrics of the XIVth Century.* Oxford, 1924. Rev. by G. V. Smithers, 1957.

———, ed. *Religious Lyrics of the XVth Century.* Oxford, 1939.

Davies, R. T., ed. *Medieval English Lyrics.* Evanston, Ill., 1967.

Greene, Richard Leighton, ed. *The Early English Carols.* Oxford, 1935.

Morris, Richard, ed. *An Old English Miscellany.* Early English Text Society No. 49 (1872).

Person, Henry A., ed. *Cambridge Middle English Lyrics.* Seattle, 1962.

Robbins, Rossell Hope, ed. "The Findern Anthology." *PMLA* 69(1954): 610–642.

———, ed. *Historical Poems of the XIVth and XVth Centuries.* New York, 1959.

———, ed. "Popular Prayers in Middle English Verse." *MP* 36(1939): 337–350.

———, ed. *Secular Lyrics of the XIVth and XVth Centuries.* 2nd ed. Oxford, 1955.

———. "Wall Verses at Launceston Priory," *Archiv für das Studium der Neueren Sprachen und Literaturen* 200(1963): 338–343.

Stevick, Robert D., ed. *One Hundred Middle English Lyrics.* Indianapolis, 1964.

Wilson, R. M. *The Lost Literature of Medieval England.* London, 1952.

2. Studies Bearing on the Middle English Lyric

Abel, Patricia Anna. "Imagery in the English Medieval Secular Lyric in the XIIIth and XIVth Centuries." *DA* 17(1957): 2258.

Anonymous. "Review of *Medieval English Lyrics*," by R. T. Davies. *TLS*, 23 April 1964, p. 344.

Appleton, Sarah Sherman. "Theology and Poetry in the Middle English Lyric." *DA* 22(1962): 4002.

Brandl, Alois. "Spielmannsverhältnisse in frühmittelenglischer Zeit." *Forschungen und Charakteristiken*. Berlin, 1936.

Chambers, E. K. *English Literature at the Close of the Middle Ages.* Oxford, 1947.

Chaytor, Henry J. *From Script to Print: An Introduction to Medieval Vernacular Literature*. Cambridge, 1945.
——, *The Troubadours and England*. Cambridge, 1923.
Clark, Donald L. "Rhetoric and the Literature of the English Middle Ages." *Quarterly Journal of Speech* 45(1959): 19–28.
Conley, John Allen. "Four Studies in Aureate Terms." *DA* 17(1957): 353.
Cross, J. E. "The *Sayings of St. Bernard* and *Ubi Sount Qui Ante Nos Fuerount.*" *RES*, n.s., 9(1958): 1–7.
Curry, Jane L. "Imagery in the Middle English Secular Lyric: the Love Lyric." M.A. dissertation, Stanford University, 1962.
Degginger, Stuart Hugh Louis. "The Earliest Middle English Lyrics, 1150–1325; An Investigation of the Influence of Latin, Provençal, and French." *DA* 14(1954): 107–108.
Dronke, Peter. *Medieval Latin and the Rise of the European Love-Lyric*. Oxford, 1966.
Enkvist, Nils Erik. *The Seasons of the Year: Chapters on a Motif from Beowulf to the Shepherd's Calendar*. Commentationes Humanarum Litterarum, Vol. XXII. Helsingfors, 1957.
Fifield, Merle. "Thirteenth-Century Lyrics and the Alliterative Tradition." *JEGP* 62(1963): 111–118.
Greene, Richard L. " 'The Maid of the Moor' in the *Red Book of Ossory*." *Speculum* 27(1952): 504–506.
——. " 'The Port of Peace': Not Death but God." *MLN* 69 (1954): 307–309.
Hodgart, M. J. C. "Medieval Lyrics and the Ballad." In *The Age of Chaucer*, Boris Ford, ed. Harmondsworth, 1962.
Hogan, Clare. "A Critical Study of the Middle English Lyrics of Br. Museum Ms. Harley 2253." *DA* 23(1962): 1350.
Jackson, William T. H. "The Medieval Pastourelle as a Satirical Genre." *PQ* 31 (1952): 156–170.
Kane, George. *Middle English Literature*. London, 1951.
Ker, W. P. *Medieval English Literature*. London, 1912.
Kinney, Thomas Leroy. "English Verse of Complaint, 1250–1400." *DA* 20(1959): 1767–1768.
Lewis, C. S. "The Fifteenth-Century Heroic Line." In *Essays and Studies by Members of the English Association*, 24(1938): 28–41.
Malone, Kemp, and Baugh, Albert C. *The Middle Ages. A Literary History of England*, ed. Albert C. Baugh, 2nd. ed., vol. 1. New York, 1967.
Malone, Kemp. "Notes on Middle English Lyrics." *ELH* 2(1935): 58–65.
Manning, Stephen. *Wisdom and Number: Toward a Critical Appraisal of the Middle English Lyric*. Lincoln, Nebr., 1962.
McGarry, Sr. Loretta. *The Holy Eucharist in Middle English Homiletic and Devotional Verse*. Washington, D.C., 1936.
Mendenhall, John Cooper. *Aureate Terms: A Study in the Literary Diction of the Fifteenth Century*. Lancaster, Pa., 1919.

Menner, Robert J. "Notes on Middle English Lyrics." *MLN* 55(1940): 243–249.

Meroney, Howard. "Line-Notes on the Early English Lyric." *MLN* 62(1947): 184–187.

Miller, Catharine K. "The Early English Carol." *Renaissance News* 3 (1950): 61–64.

Moore, Arthur K. *The Secular Lyric in Middle English.* Lexington, Ky., 1951.

Müller, Alexander. *Mittelenglische geistliche und weltliche Lyrik des XIII. Jahrhunderts: nach Motiven und Formen.* Halle, 1911.

Owst, G. R. *Literature and Pulpit in Medieval England.* Cambridge, 1933.

Patterson, Frank A. *The Middle English Penitential Lyric.* New York, 1911.

Reed, Edward Bliss. " 'Wynter Wakeneth al my Care.' " *MLN* 43(1928): 81–84.

Rees, Elinor C. "A Study of the Portrayal of Moods and Emotions in Early Vernacular Lyrical Poetry." *Stanford University Bulletin, Abstracts of Dissertations* 11(1935–1936): 57–63.

Reiss, Edmund. "A Critical Approach to the Middle English Lyric." *College English* 27(1966): 373–379.

Robbins, Rossell Hope. "The Authors of the Middle English Religious Lyrics." *JEGP* 39 (1940): 230–238.

———. "The Burden in the Carols." *MLN* 57(1942): 16–22.

———. " 'Consilium domini in eternum manet' (Harley Ms. 2252)." *Studia Neophilologica* 26(1954): 58–64.

———. "The Earliest Carols and the Franciscans." *MLN* 53(1938): 239–245.

———. "English Almanacks of the Fifteenth Century." *PQ* 18(1939): 321–331.

———. "An Epitaph for Duke Humphrey (1447)." *Neuphilologische Mitteilungen* 56 (1955): 241–249.

———. "Friar Herebert and the Carol." *Anglia* 75(1957): 194–198.

———. "The Gurney Series of Religious Lyrics." *PMLA* 54 (1939): 369–390.

———. "Middle English Carols as Processional Hymns." *SP* 56(1959): 559–582.

———. "Middle English Versions of 'Criste qui lux es et dies.' " *Harvard Theological Review* 47(1954): 55–63.

———. "An Unkind Mistress (Lambeth Ms. 432)." *MLN* 69(1954): 552–558.

———. "Wall Verses at Launceston Priory." *Archiv für das Studium der Neueren Sprachen und Literaturen* 200(1963): 338–343.

Sahlin, Margit. *Etude sur la carole médiévale: l'origine du mot et ses rapports avec l'église.* Uppsala, 1940.

Schirmer, Walter F. "Dichter und Publikum zu Ende des 15. Jahrhunderts in England." *Zeitschrift für Ästhetik und Allgemeine Kunstwissenschaft* 28(1934): 209–224.

Schoeck, R. J. "Alliterative Assonance in Harley Ms. 2253." *ES* 32 (1951): 68–70.

————. Review of Arthur K. Moore's *Secular Lyrics in Middle English*. *Speculum* 27(1952): 114–116.

Sikora, Ruta. "The Structural Simplicity of the Early Middle English Lyric: Three Examples." *Kwartalnik Neofilologiczny* 11(1964): 233–242.

Speirs, John. *Medieval English Poetry: The Non-Chaucerian Tradition*. London, 1957.

Spitzer, Leo. "*Explication de Texte* Applied to Three Great Middle English Poems." *Archivum Linguisticum* 3(1949): 137–165.

Stemmler, Theo. "Zur Verfasserfrage der Charles D'Orleans zugeschriebenen englischen Gedichte." *Anglia* 82(1964): 458–473.

Stevick, Robert D. "The Criticism of Middle English Lyrics." *MP* 64(1966): 103–117.

Taylor, George C. "The English 'Planctus Mariae.'" *MP* 4(1907): 605–637.

————. "The Relation of the English *Corpus Christi* Play to the Middle English Religious Lyric." *MP* 5(1907): 1–39.

Tuve, Rosemond. *Seasons and Months: Studies in a Tradition of Middle English Poetry*. Paris, 1933.

Waldron, Ronald A. "Oral-Formulaic Technique and Middle English Alliterative Poetry." *Speculum* 32(1957): 792–804.

Wehrle, William O. *The Macaronic Hymn Tradition in Medieval English Literature*. Washington, D.C., 1933.

White, Natalie Elizabeth. "The English Liturgical Refrain Lyric before 1450, with Special Reference to the Fourteenth Century." *Abstracts of Dissertations*, Stanford University 20(1944–1945): 35–37.

Wolpers, Theodor. "Geschichte der englischen Marienlyrik." *Anglia* 69(1950): 3–88.

Woolf, Rosemary. *The English Religious Lyric in the Middle Ages*. Oxford, 1968.

————. "The Theme of Christ the Lover-Knight in Medieval English Literature." *RES*, n.s., 13(1962): 1–16.

Index of First Lines of Middle English Lyrics

This index includes only Middle English poems that have been quoted in full, except for two items marked by daggers. The parentheses include the standard edition of the poem and its number, if any, in that edition (see the list of abbreviations, p. xv). Following the parentheses, the principal manuscript in which that poem occurs is identified. For carols, only the first line of the first stanza is given, not the first line of the burden. The runic letter þ is indexed as *Th*.